GLOBAL VIEWPOINTS

Disasters

Other Books of Related Interest:

At Issue Series

Are Natural Disasters Increasing?

Solar Storms

Current Controversies Series

Oil Spills

Opposing Viewpoints Series

Natural Disasters

GLOBALVIEWPOINTS

Disasters

Diane Andrews Henningfeld, Book Editor

GREENHAVEN PRESS
A part of Gale, Cengage Learning

GALE
CENGAGE Learning·

Detroit • New York • San Francisco • New Haven, Conn • Waterville, Maine • London

Elizabeth Des Chenes, *Director, Content Strategy*
Cynthia Sanner, *Publisher*
Douglas Dentino, *Manager, New Product*

For more information, contact:
Greenhaven Press
27500 Drake Rd.
Farmington Hills, MI 48331-3535
Or you can visit our Internet site at gale.cengage.com

For product information and technology assistance, contact us at

Gale Customer Support, 1-800-877-4253
For permission to use material from this text or product, submit all requests online at
www.cengage.com/permissions

Further permissions questions can be emailed to permissionrequest@cengage.com

Articles in Greenhaven Press anthologies are often edited for length to meet page requirements. In addition, original titles of these works are changed to clearly present the main thesis and to explicitly indicate the author's opinion. Every effort is made to ensure that Greenhaven Press accurately reflects the original intent of the authors. Every effort has been made to trace the owners of copyrighted material.

Cover image copyright © A. S. Zain/Shutterstock.com.

LIBRARY OF CONGRESS CATALOGING-IN-PUBLICATION DATA

Disasters / Diane Andrews Henningfeld, book editor.
    pages cm -- (Global viewpoints)
    Includes bibliographical references and index.
    ISBN 978-0-7377-6262-4 (hardcover) -- ISBN 978-0-7377-6438-3 (pbk.)
    1. Disaster relief. 2. Disasters. 3. Natural disasters. 4. Emergency management. I.
Henningfeld, Diane Andrews.
    HV553.D374 2014
    363.34--dc23

                                                                    2013026136

Printed in the United States of America
 1 2 3 4 5   18 17 16 15 14

Contents

A presidential commission examined the causes of the devastating oil spill in the Gulf of Mexico that occurred when the BP Macondo well exploded in 2010. The commission concluded that the explosion and subsequent environmental disaster were caused by identifiable mistakes made by BP, Halliburton, and Transocean.

Chapter 2: Disasters, Social Issues, and Politics

Survivors of the 1984 Bhopal gas leak in India, the worst industrial disaster in history, suffer ongoing health and reproductive problems. Many women, though poor and ill-educated, have banded together to demand justice for the accident.

Chapter 3: Disaster Preparedness

In an interview, a climate hazard expert argues that many lives could be saved if governments could turn to a central worldwide database containing information on natural disasters.

Chapter 4: Disaster Response and Aftermath

The World Bank draws on lessons from past disaster response to build an effective plan for Haiti relief after the devastating 2010 earthquake.

Foreword

> "The problems of all of humanity can only be solved by all of humanity."
> —Swiss author Friedrich Dürrenmatt

Global interdependence has become an undeniable reality. Mass media and technology have increased worldwide access to information and created a society of global citizens. Understanding and navigating this global community is a challenge, requiring a high degree of information literacy and a new level of learning sophistication.

Building on the success of its flagship series, Opposing Viewpoints, Greenhaven Press has created the Global Viewpoints series to examine a broad range of current, often controversial topics of worldwide importance from a variety of international perspectives. Providing students and other readers with the information they need to explore global connections and think critically about worldwide implications, each Global Viewpoints volume offers a panoramic view of a topic of widespread significance.

Drugs, famine, immigration—a broad, international treatment is essential to do justice to social, environmental, health, and political issues such as these. Junior high, high school, and early college students, as well as general readers, can all use Global Viewpoints anthologies to discern the complexities relating to each issue. Readers will be able to examine unique national perspectives while, at the same time, appreciating the interconnectedness that global priorities bring to all nations and cultures.

Material in each volume is selected from a diverse range of sources, including journals, magazines, newspapers, nonfiction books, speeches, government documents, pamphlets, organization newsletters, and position papers. Global Viewpoints is truly global, with material drawn primarily from international sources available in English and secondarily from US sources with extensive international coverage.

Features of each volume in the Global Viewpoints series include:

- An **annotated table of contents** that provides a brief summary of each essay in the volume, including the name of the country or area covered in the essay.

- An **introduction** specific to the volume topic.

- A **world map** to help readers locate the countries or areas covered in the essays.

- For each viewpoint, an **introduction** that contains notes about the author and source of the viewpoint explains why material from the specific country is being presented, summarizes the main points of the viewpoint, and offers three **guided reading questions** to aid in understanding and comprehension.

- **For further discussion** questions that promote critical thinking by asking the reader to compare and contrast aspects of the viewpoints or draw conclusions about perspectives and arguments.

- A worldwide list of **organizations to contact** for readers seeking additional information.

- A **periodical bibliography** for each chapter and a **bibliography of books** on the volume topic to aid in further research.

- A comprehensive **subject index** to offer access to people, places, events, and subjects cited in the text, with the countries covered in the viewpoints highlighted.

Global Viewpoints is designed for a broad spectrum of readers who want to learn more about current events, history, political science, government, international relations, economics, environmental science, world cultures, and sociology—students doing research for class assignments or debates, teachers and faculty seeking to supplement course materials, and others wanting to understand current issues better. By presenting how people in various countries perceive the root causes, current consequences, and proposed solutions to worldwide challenges, Global Viewpoints volumes offer readers opportunities to enhance their global awareness and their knowledge of cultures worldwide.

Introduction

"Disasters are a complex mix of natural hazards and human action."

—Ben Wisner,
Piers Blaikie, Terry Cannon,
and Ian Davis, At Risk: Natural
Hazards, People's Vulnerability
and Disasters, *2nd ed. London:
Taylor and Frances, 2004*

When most people hear the word *disaster*, they think of large-scale cataclysmic events, such as an earthquake, a tidal wave, or a hurricane, and with good reason. These events cause tremendous upheaval in the lives of those affected. As writers from the Johns Hopkins Bloomberg School of Public Health note, "The word *disaster* implies a sudden overwhelming and unforeseen event."

However, disasters are much more complicated than the word might suggest for most people. Rather than a single event, disasters often occur as the result of many forces that come into play before, during, and after a sudden event. In addition, disasters can be slow to unfold, occurring over months and even years. For example, drought can lead to crop failures, which in turn can lead to hunger and malnutrition. Not every drought becomes a disaster, but if a drought continues for a long enough period and food sources become increasingly rare, famine will set in, leading to death from malnutrition and opportunistic diseases. Famine is a disaster in slow motion, as opposed to a sudden overwhelming event, often years in the making and years in the recovery. The Great Famine in Ireland, for example, began with a plant disease known as potato blight that first appeared in 1845. By 1846, people began dying, and they continued to die for another five years before conditions improved.

Likewise, another disaster that continues to unfold slowly is the AIDS pandemic that has rampaged around the world with disastrous consequences since the 1980s. According to the World Health Organization, thirty million people have died since the illness was first discovered. This figure does not reflect the multifaceted nature of the tragedy, however. In addition to the deaths, as of 2010, another thirty million people were living with the disease, and millions of children had been orphaned. In 2010, 69 percent of all those who died of AIDS lived in Africa. Social issues of poverty, gender, and race complicate the natural disaster of disease.

Most disaster experts distinguish between natural hazards and human-caused events as triggering forces in disasters. Natural hazards are events occurring naturally on, under, or above the earth's surface. Thus, drought, floods, storms, and earthquakes are all natural hazards, as are volcanoes and limnic eruptions, a rare but deadly occurrence when methane gases build up under a lake and suddenly explode. On the other hand, accidental or intentional human-caused disasters result in death and destruction of the environment. Events such as the 1986 Chernobyl nuclear accident in Russia, which led to the permanent evacuation of thousands of people, and the 1984 Bhopal gas leak tragedy in India, which killed some sixteen thousand people, are examples of human-caused catastrophes.

These distinctions, however, are not as clear-cut as they may seem. Often a natural hazard can become a catastrophic disaster because of the actions, or inaction, of humans. A striking example of this is Hurricane Katrina, a major storm that hit the US Gulf Coast in 2005. The storm was a natural hazard; hurricanes often enter the Gulf of Mexico, bringing with them high winds, storm surges, torrential rains, and flooding. This is a part of a natural cycle. Because large numbers of humans chose to settle in places that were essentially floodplains and likely to be inundated by storm surges, however, Katrina was devastating for those who lived there.

Further, in the case of Katrina, inadequate preparation and slow response by the New Orleans city government, the state of Louisiana, and the US government resulted in more human misery than was necessary. These governments did not adequately prepare for a hurricane of Katrina's power. Evacuation plans were not well developed and many poor people were trapped in a city flooded by rising waters, demonstrating how the social condition of poverty can make a group of people more vulnerable to a natural hazard. In addition, the human-engineered levee system that was supposed to protect New Orleans residents broke. As a result, floodwaters rushed in on sections of New Orleans where large numbers of African American and poor residents lived. Race and poverty became social factors that complicated the response to the disaster.

Katrina shocked the nation, and Congress appointed a special committee to investigate how a natural hazard became an unmitigated disaster. Its findings, published as "A Failure of Initiative: Final Report of the Select Bipartisan Committee to Investigate the Preparation for and Response to Hurricane Katrina" in 2006, severely criticized the local, state, and federal governments for their failure to act. The committee wrote, "The failure of complete evacuations led to preventable deaths, great suffering, and further delays in relief." In addition, the committee found failures to adequately plan for and respond to a large-scale emergency at all levels of government. The report was scathing.

Discussions about whether New Orleans should be rebuilt, how it should be rebuilt, how to help New Orleans residents return to the city, how to restore power, and how to rebuild the levee system all became part of a tremendously complicated political and social debate—a debate that has continued for years after the storm. The effects of Katrina continue to haunt New Orleans and will likely do so over the coming decades.

Natural events, such as drought and desertification, can lead to the worst of all situations: armed conflict, as people struggle to find enough food and water. Ben Wisner, Piers Blaikie, Terry Cannon, and Ian Davis write, "During the 1980s and 1990s, war in Africa, the post-war displacement of people and the destruction of infrastructure made the rebuilding of lives already shattered by drought virtually impossible." It is difficult to overemphasize the catastrophe of war. As experts from the Bloomberg School of Public Health write, "Armed conflicts, often called Complex Humanitarian Emergencies, are the worst disasters that can befall populations." Millions of civilians have been killed and large areas of land have been ruined by armed conflict, and the damage caused by conflict lives on for decades and through generations. War in all forms, whether precipitated by a natural event, such as drought, or a political event, such as an ideological crusade, kills more people and damages the environment more than all other hazards combined.

The chapters that follow offer an overview of the many causes of disaster in all their complexities; an examination of the social and cultural dimensions of disasters including poverty, gender, and politics; a review of natural disaster preparedness; and a look at both effective and ineffective responses to disasters.

GLOBALVIEWPOINTS

Causes of Disasters

Climate Change May Increase Natural Disasters Worldwide

World Health Organization

In the following viewpoint, writers from the World Health Organization (WHO) present evidence that the climate of the earth is changing. In addition, they argue that climate change will place many people at risk for death, injury, or illness. They project that the number of severe storms including cyclones and hurricanes, droughts followed by food shortages, and floods will increase as the climate warms. Moreover, they offer data suggesting that the increase in catastrophic weather events is already happening. WHO is the public health arm of the United Nations.

As you read, consider the following questions:

1. What are some human health problems that WHO attributes to heat waves?

2. What summer 2003 event is cited in the viewpoint as causing seventy thousand more deaths in western Europe than would otherwise be expected for that time of year?

3. By what percentage does WHO project the frequency of category 5 storms to increase within eighty years?

The basic facts are now firmly established. The earth is warming rapidly, mainly because of emissions of greenhouse gases caused by human activity. If current patterns of fossil fuel use, development and population growth continue, this will lead to ongoing climate change, with serious effects on the environment and, consequently, on human lives and health. . . .

Climate Change May Cause Health Disasters

Climate change will affect, in profoundly adverse ways, some of the most fundamental prerequisites for good health: clean air and water, sufficient food, adequate shelter and freedom from disease. The global climate is now changing faster than at any point in human civilization, and many of the effects on health will be acutely felt. The most severe risks are to developing countries, with negative implications for the achievement of the health-related Millennium Development Goals [MDGs] and for health equity.

Extreme air temperatures and air pollution are hazardous to health. Heat waves are a direct contributor to deaths from cardiovascular and respiratory disease, particularly among elderly people. High temperatures also raise the levels of ozone and other air pollutants that exacerbate cardiovascular and respiratory disease, and pollen and other aeroallergens that trigger asthma.

Floods, droughts and contaminated water raise disease risk. More variable precipitation is occurring, with an increase in the frequency and intensity of both floods and droughts. At the same time, higher temperatures are hastening rates of evaporation of surface waters and melting the glaciers that provide fresh water for many populations. Lack of fresh water compromises hygiene, thus increasing rates of diarrhoeal disease. In extreme cases, water scarcity results in drought and famine. Too much water, in the form of floods, causes contamination of freshwater supplies and also creates opportunities for breeding of disease-carrying insects such as mosquitoes.

Expected increases in the frequency and severity of flooding and storms will result in the destruction of homes, medical facilities and other essential services, impacting particularly on people in slums and other marginal living conditions.

Climatic effects on agriculture threatens increasing malnutrition. Rising temperatures and changing patterns of rainfall are projected to decrease crop yields in many developing countries, stressing food supplies. For populations that depend on subsistence farming, or do not have sufficient income to buy food, this situation is expected to translate directly into wider prevalence of malnutrition. In turn, malnutrition and undernutrition increase the severity of many infectious diseases, particularly among children.

More extreme and variable climate can destroy homes, communities and lives. Expected increases in the frequency and severity of flooding and storms will result in the destruction of homes, medical facilities and other essential services, impacting particularly on people in slums and other marginal living conditions. Gradual sea level rise, particularly coupled with stronger storm surges, will tend to lead to more frequent and more severe coastal flooding. The consequent destruction of homes and communities will eventually force unprotected populations to seek safer ground, often increasing environmental and social pressures in their new locations.

Climate change brings new challenges to the control of infectious diseases. Many of the major killer diseases transmitted by water and contaminated food, and by insect vectors are

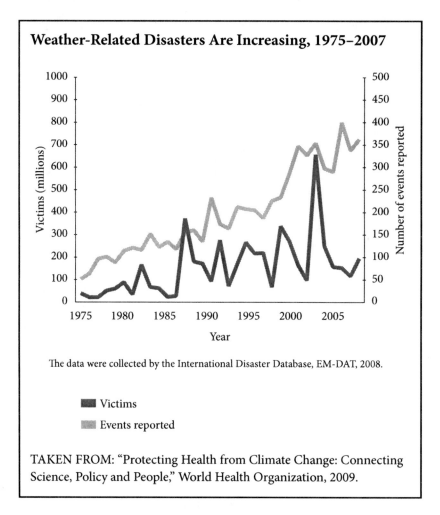

Weather-Related Disasters Are Increasing, 1975–2007

The data were collected by the International Disaster Database, EM-DAT, 2008.

■ Victims

▨ Events reported

TAKEN FROM: "Protecting Health from Climate Change: Connecting Science, Policy and People," World Health Organization, 2009.

highly sensitive to climatic conditions and weather extremes. Climate change threatens to slow, halt or reverse current progress against many of these infections.

Not all of the effects of climate change will be harmful, but on balance health damages are projected to outweigh the benefits. A warmer climate is expected to bring benefits to some populations, including reduced mortality and morbidity in winter and greater local food production, particularly in northern high latitudes. However, projections by WHO [World Health Organization] and IPCC [Intergovernmental Panel on Climate

Change] suggest that the negative effects of climate change on health are greater and are more strongly supported by evidence than are the possible benefits. In addition, the negative effects are concentrated on poor populations that already have compromised health prospects, thus widening the inequality gap between the most and the least privileged.

Natural Disasters Are Rising

Globally, the number of reported weather-related natural disasters is mounting rapidly. Reports of natural catastrophes have more than tripled since the 1960s. In 2007, 14 out of 15 "flash appeals" for emergency humanitarian assistance were for floods, droughts and storms—five times higher than in any previous year [according to United Nations aid chief John Holmes].

More numerous reports of natural disasters are partly due to population growth in high-risk areas, but it is possible that climate change is also a contributing factor. The last few decades have seen rapid growth in populations living in floodplains and coastal areas, particularly in developing country cities, placing more people in the path of weather-related natural disasters. At the same time, climate change has furthered the probability of extreme high temperatures and has probably contributed to more frequent and extreme precipitation events and more intense tropical cyclone activity [according to the IPCC]. Together, these trends will increase weather-related hazards to human health.

Extreme heat. Studies from around the world have shown that temperatures above a locally specific threshold result in higher mortality rates. The extended hot summer of 2003 in Europe produced sustained record high temperatures which resulted in markedly higher death rates, particularly among the elderly population. In total, it has been estimated that 70,000 more deaths occurred in western Europe during that extreme summer than would have been expected for the time of year. Continuing global warming and possible increases in temperature variability will make such events more frequent—and more severe. It is expected that European summer temperatures as high as those experienced in 2003 will be the norm by the middle of the century.

Globally, the number of reported weather-related natural disasters is mounting rapidly.

Floods and droughts. Even small changes in average precipitation can have a very large effect on the extremes of rainfall events that cause either flooding or drought, already the most frequent and deadly forms of natural disasters. For example, studies have shown that human influence on the global climate is likely to make what would currently be considered a "very wet winter" in the United Kingdom, or a "very wet summer" in the South Asian monsoon region, about five times more frequent by the second half of this century [according to T.N. Palmer and J. Ralsanen writing in *Nature*]. Globally, climate change is likely to widen the area affected by drought, with particularly severe impacts in areas that are already water-stressed. These trends will impact on lives and on health. Floods cause drownings and physical injuries; heighten the risk of diseases transmitted through water, insect vectors and rodents; damage homes; and disrupt the supply of essential medical and health services. The number of floods reported globally is rising rapidly—much more rapidly than disasters unrelated to weather conditions. Droughts increase the risk of food shortages and malnutrition. They also increase the risk of diseases spread by contaminated food and water.

Tropical storms. Extreme winds, particularly in the tropical regions, bring death and destruction. There is evidence for a marked increase in the numbers of the most extreme cyclones in recent decades, and this trend is likely to continue. Studies indicate that a doubling of the level of carbon dioxide in the atmosphere, expected within about 80 years, will result in an increase of only about 6% in average cyclone wind speed but of 300% in the frequency of the largest (category 5) storms.

Famine in Africa Is the Result of a Natural Disaster

Alhagie Jobe

In the following viewpoint, Alhagie Jobe reports that drought is causing a famine in the Horn of Africa, an area of the continent that includes the countries of Eritrea, Djibouti, Ethiopia, and Somalia. He asserts that Somalia has been particularly devastated, with the deaths of about twenty-nine thousand children under the age of five. In 2010 the region suffered from the driest rainy season in sixty years, at which point the Food and Agriculture Organization of the United Nations (FAO) issued a famine warning. While drought is the cause of the famine, conflict in the region has made conditions even worse.

As you read, consider the following questions:

1. What is Somalia's malnutrition rate, according to CARE?

2. According to the viewpoint, what percentage of crops has been lost in Ethiopia and Eritrea?

3. The viewpoint asserts that immediate relief is the most pressing issue but also urges the world to promote what?

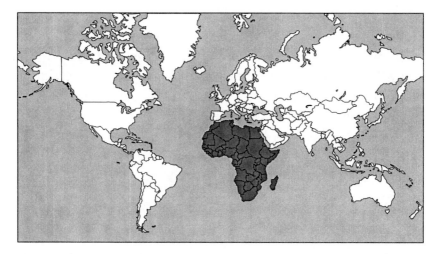

Drought is today causing the evil famine in the Horn of Africa worse than ever, though the phenomenon is not new in the world's poorest continent. In 2003, the then WFP [World Food Programme] executive director James Morris referred to famine in Africa as an unprecedented crisis needing unprecedented response.

He warned "the magnitude of the disaster has not been fully grasped by the international community." Eight years later, the international community is still grappling with the same situation.

The Disaster of Famine

Today, hunger and conflict continue to claim thousands of lives in the Horn of Africa. However, the call for a global response is getting louder.

Images of starving Somalis have shaken the conscience of the world: stomachs flattened by hunger, sagging flesh and noses dripping in mucus, fed on by opportunistic toilet flies. And death is lurking. This is the picture of many of the living in Somalia, who look to humanity for help.

Jerry Rawlings, former Ghanaian president, wept inconsolably on Channel 4, a British television channel, as he recounted his experience after visiting Somalia in July [2011]. Mr. Rawlings, who is the African Union high representative to the drought- and war-ravaged country, begged the world for a "miracle of compassion" and urged it to "focus on tackling this unfolding catastrophe if we are to prevent further needless loss of life."

The United Nations [UN] in July officially declared famine in five regions of Somalia—Mogadishu, Afgoye, Middle Shabelle, Lower Shabelle and Southern Bakool. Tens of thousands of shallow graves litter these regions. So far some 29,000 children under the age of five are among the buried. By mid-August, 400,000 Somalis had made lucky escapes to the Dadaab refugee camp in northeastern Kenya, now reportedly the world's largest.

The UN Food and Agriculture Organization (FAO), which monitors trends in global food prices, adds that up to 1,500 people move daily across the border to the Dadaab camp. Somalia's malnutrition rate is 50 per cent, the highest in the world, according to CARE, a humanitarian charity.

Images of starving Somalis have shaken the conscience of the world: stomachs flattened by hunger, sagging flesh, and noses dripping in mucus. . . . And death is lurking.

UN Secretary-General Ban Ki-moon sounded the alarm bells in early July, prodding the world to act speedily to prevent thousands more from dying. Mr. Ban's widely published op-ed narrated the story of Halima Omar, a Somali woman, who lost four of her six children. Halima said: "There is nothing worse than seeing your own child die because you cannot feed him."

Drought Plus Conflict Is Deadly

Somalia is in particularly dire straits because conflict, drought and high global food prices have exacerbated the humanitarian situation. The Al-Shabaab militia group, with links to Al-Qaida, controls southern Somalia and is preventing aid from reaching 3.6 million people (nearly half the population), of whom about 1.4 million are severely affected by the drought.

According to the Human Rights Watch, the militia group considers aid agencies as "infidels," adding that "abuses by Al-Shabaab and pro-government forces have vastly multiplied the suffering from Somalia's famine."

The WFP is currently investigating a recent theft of food aid, with accusing fingers already pointed at both pro-government forces and elements of Al-Shabaab.

The entire Horn of Africa is experiencing an acute food crisis. According to the UN boss, 12.4 million people in the region are in desperate need of food aid. Uganda has had four successive poor harvests.

In Kenya maize crops are 28 per cent of their normal average; only Nairobi, Mombasa and Kisumu have experienced rainfall, and 80 per cent of the country is semi-arid or arid. In Ethiopia and Eritrea crop losses are up to 75 per cent in some areas. And skyrocketing global food prices affect import-dependent Djibouti and Somalia.

The UN's World Food Programme (WFP) is dropping vitamin-fortified biscuits in the most affected areas, literally rescuing the hunger-stricken from the brink of death. Yet, there are thousands more too weak to chew the biscuits. This category must first receive nutrients by intravenous means to stay alive.

Aid inflows are currently short of what is required to stem the tide of deaths. In August, only 48 per cent of the $2.5 billion needed had been received, says Mark Bowden, the UN coordinator in Somalia.

"We're worried that people are going to die in the next month or so and inevitably more areas will slip into famine." There is urgent need for the remaining $1.3 billion. The [UN] Security Council has urged members to contribute to the UN consolidated appeal for Somalia and expressed "serious concern that the appeal is not fully funded."

The US has led in donations. Secretary of State Hillary Clinton announced on CBS, a television network, that US support for relief efforts has topped $500 million. "The situation breaks my heart," Ms. Clinton said of Somalia, promising that US support will continue in diverse ways.

Kenyan bloggers, Kenya 4 Kenyans, have taken advantage of the Internet and mobile phone technology to raise awareness of the Somalia famine. Already, they have raked in €10 million to support victims.

Drought Warnings Were Issued

The unfolding catastrophe did not come as a surprise—at least not to the FAO. In August 2010, the FAO issued a drought warning. And between October and December 2010, characterized as the driest season in 60 years, the FAO again warned of calamitous crop prospects for the region.

The international community has been slow to respond, prompting Oxfam, a UK [United Kingdom] charity, to describe the situation as "a catastrophic breakdown in the world's collective responsibility to act."

The occurrence of widespread, severe drought in Africa once again underscored the vulnerability of developing societies to drought.

The FAO explained that humanitarian crises such as worsening drought in the Horn of Africa are considered "slow-onset," and generally get "less financial and media attention than other disasters and tragedies, such as the earthquake in Haiti or the floods in Pakistan."

The UN, many governments across the world and celebrities are mobilizing to save lives in the Horn of Africa. The immediate goal is to stop the dying. But even if that is achieved, it will provide at best temporary relief. Climate forecasts for the next months are not encouraging, as the dry conditions are expected to continue, with temperatures rising even higher. Food prices will continue to rise, with Oxfam predicting they will double in the next 20 years.

What should be done: As more hands get on deck to tackle the current crisis, efforts also should target the longer term, including providing implements and other logistical support so that farmers can improve their future harvests in Africa.

However, even as farmers are ready to toil, they are asking when the rains will fall. And for some parts in Africa, it is also when they will not have to flee in fright of hunger and the militia. Until then, the Horn of Africa remains what the BBC aptly describes as a "vision of hell."

The occurrence of widespread, severe drought in Africa once again underscored the vulnerability of developing societies to drought. These recent droughts in Africa have emphasized the need for more research on the causes as well as the impacts of drought and the need for additional planning to help mitigate the possible worst effects of future droughts.

Drought has been the subject of a great deal of systematic study, particularly reconstructions of drought history, computations of drought frequency and, to a lesser extent, investigations of first- second-, and even third-order impacts of drought on society.

While immediate relief is the most pressing issue to save lives, the world should work to promote long-term sustainability, especially in terms of access to clean water.

This includes expanding existing wells, building new water sources like rainwater catchment systems and building better irrigation systems to help save crops from future droughts; protecting livestock, seed distribution, providing vaccinations, providing stabilizing centers for severely acute malnourished children, etc.

Famine in Africa Is Caused by Humans, Not Nature

Thomas Keneally

In the following viewpoint, Thomas Keneally argues that modern famines are rarely caused by drought. He offers as evidence the situation in Australia where droughts occur frequently, but no one starves. He asserts, rather, that corrupt governments, grain merchants, and militant groups cause famine. Corrupt governments fail to plan for food shortages and protect their citizens. Grain merchants hoard food so that prices will rise and increase their wealth. Militant groups such as Al-Shabaab in Somalia prevent aid from reaching starving people. Thus, famine is a human-made disaster. Keneally is an Australian writer of fiction and nonfiction.

As you read, consider the following questions:

1. On what did Rev. Thomas Robert Malthus blame the Irish potato famine, according to Keneally?

2. What percentage of Korean children were malnourished in 2010, according to Keneally?

3. What should aid agencies invite citizens of the world to do in times of famine, according to Keneally?

Thomas Keneally, "War and Corruption, Not Droughts, Are Responsible for Famines," *Globe and Mail*, September 2, 2011. By arrangement with the Licensor, Thomas Keneally, c/- Curtis Brown (Aust) Pty Ltd.

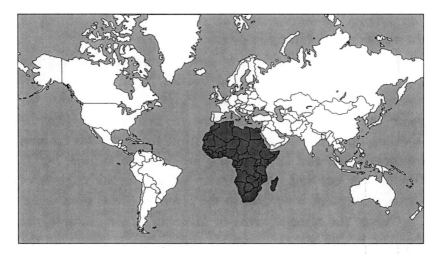

I have never quite believed that simplistic formula invoked in so many modern famines: "caused by a severe drought."

Not that there isn't a severe drought now in southern Somalia, neighbouring Ethiopia and parts of Kenya. There undeniably is. Last October to December [2010], rains did not appear at all in the area. The March–April rains this year [2011] were late. My skepticism arises, though, because I come from perhaps the driest continent on Earth, which has suffered recurrent droughts from earliest settler experience, including the El Niño–influenced drought that seemed to run nearly nonstop from the early 1990s to last year. Many of our farmers were forced off land their families had held for generations.

There has always been drought-induced anguish in the Australian bush. But no one starves. Malnutrition, undeniably, and particularly in indigenous communities, but no famine.

Famines Do Not Occur in Functioning Democracies

How is it the citizens of drought-stricken homelands in Somalia and the "triangle of death" have none of the guarantees my drought-stricken compatriots have? It's because, as the famed aphorism of Nobel Prize–winning economist Amartya

Sen puts it, "no famine has ever taken place in the history of the world in a functioning democracy."

Similarly, an Irish friend of mine, a respected historian of famine named Cormac Ó Gráda, writes, "Agency is more important than a food-production shortfall. Mars counts for more than Malthus." In contrast to Rev. Thomas Robert Malthus, the 19th-century population theorist who blamed overpopulation and land overuse for the Irish famine, Mr. Ó Gráda, sees war and other human actions as the engines of famine. His point is evident in the Horn of Africa now.

One of the affected areas of Ethiopia is, for example, the Ogaden, whose people consider themselves kinsmen of the Somalis and are similarly Muslim. It is in their territory that conflict between the Ethiopian army and Somali rebels has occurred over recent years, with many savageries and violation.

The central regime in Addis Ababa [capital of Ethiopia] has never felt kindly or acted tenderly toward the Ogadenians anyhow, nor given them a decent share of roads or clinics or schools. Is it a priority now to feed and care for them?

All famines share common qualities, a similar DNA, that reduce acts of God like drought from real causes to mere tipping or triggering mechanisms. Famines often occur where farming and grazing are suddenly disrupted to fit some ideological plan of the leaders of the country, as in [Chinese leader] Mao Zedong's Great Leap Forward in the 1950s, Ethiopia in the 1980s and North Korea repeatedly since the mid-1990s.

Famines also strike in areas where people live in hunger and malnutrition year after year. Malnutrition is a sensitivity-numbing word—it does not capture the swollen joints, flaking skin, retarded growth, porous and fragile bone, diminished height, lethargy and disabling confusion of soul that characterize it.

As it's been said, a malnourished child can still howl out; a starving one has no strength to.

As many as 60 per cent of North Korean children aged six months to seven years were malnourished in 2010, so they were set up to become the victims of famine over the past year. Once again, ideology and military priorities offer a better explanation than mere food shortage: The regime's re-evaluation of its currency wiped out the spending power of families, all to sustain itself and its army.

Similarly, southern Somalia, according to the International Committee of the Red Cross, had the highest level of child malnutrition on Earth in July this year. A few unlucky factors, and malnutrition becomes famine.

Famines often occur where farming and grazing are suddenly disrupted to fit some ideological plan of the leaders of the country.

People in that rural hinterland already lived off only a few food staples. Among some pastoral people who survive by livestock holdings, death of animals by June this year was reaching 60 per cent. The value of a cow relative to how much grain a family could buy with it had fallen by two-thirds. Grain and lentils are what farmers live off there. As with the Irish and their buttermilk and potatoes long ago, the East African diet is balanced on a two-legged stool. Still, if drought were the cause, we could just help them until the rains returned. But it's the helping that is complicated. Climate isn't the complication; humans are.

Refusing Aid Is a Political Act

The Ethiopian army invaded a civil-war-savaged Somalia in 2006 and, after a hard-fisted occupation, installed an unpopular and only partly successful transitional federal government. Assorted militias, such as the oft-mentioned Al-Shabaab ("the youth"), retained the hinterland, where conflicts, raids and molestation of citizens by both sides have been common ever since.

Al-Shabaab has been driven from Mogadishu, but it is the most commonly cited military villain in this famine. Al-Shabaab believes that many Western agencies oppose it because of its desire to make Somalia an Islamist state.

Therefore, it restricts the entry of agencies and non-governmental organizations into its area to those it considers neutral—Red Cross and Red Crescent in particular. It rules out the World Food Programme and UNICEF [United Nations Children's Fund] and agencies such as CARE. It has created its own Office for the Supervision to Regulate the Affairs of Foreign Agencies.

Agencies and aid bodies are not always without their flaws, but it is [the militant group] Al-Shabaab, not drought, that stands between the starving and the food.

There is denial that famine actually exists too. "The UN [United Nations] wants Somalia to be in famine," a spokesman, Ali Mohamud Rage, has said. "They want push pressure on us through such calls. We agree that there is hunger in some areas, but there is no famine in Somalia."

Agencies and aid bodies are not always without their flaws, but it is Al-Shabaab, not drought, that stands between the starving and the food.

Al-Shabaab not only threatens aid workers but tries to prevent and punish refugees who try to cross into so-called Christian countries such as Ethiopia and Kenya.

It must be terrifying for the men, women and children now trying to get into Kenya to find themselves surrounded by militia men emerging from the thorn trees.

Is the transitional federal government in Mogadishu an improvement or another face of the problem?

> # Early Action Could Have Mitigated the East African Food Crisis
>
> East Africa is facing the worst food crisis of the 21st century. Across Ethiopia, Somalia, and Kenya, 12 million people are in dire need of food, clean water, and basic sanitation. Loss of life on a massive scale is a very real risk, and the crisis is set to worsen over the coming months, particularly for pastoralist communities.
>
> The overall international donor response to this humanitarian crisis has been slow and inadequate. According to UN [United Nations] figures, $1bn [billion] is required to meet immediate needs. So far donors have committed less than $200m [million], leaving an $800m black hole.
>
> While severe drought has undoubtedly led to the huge scale of the disaster, this crisis has been caused by people and policies, as much as by weather patterns. If more action had been taken earlier it could have helped mitigate the severity of the current crisis. It is no coincidence that the worst affected areas are those suffering from entrenched poverty due to marginalisation and lack of investment.
>
> *Oxfam, "East Africa Food Crisis,"* Oxfam Briefing Note, *July 20, 2011. www.oxfam.org.*

It seems that it is either too venal or too powerless to prevent the plunder of aid food.

Joakim Gundel, a Kenyan assessor of aid results, says, "While helping starving people, you are also feeding the power groups who make a business out of the disaster. . . . You're saving people's lives today so they can die tomorrow."

Famine Is Caused by Humans

It seems to me that in earlier famines, this issue of human agency has not been nearly as honestly and openly discussed by journalists and officials. K'naan, the famed multitalented Canadian Somali, is rightly appalled at what he sees as a slow reaction of the world to this crisis, but the question arises whether the greater honesty about human blame is slowing the response.

The vigour and enthusiasm that came into play in the West's reaction to the Ethiopian famines of the early 1980s has not yet appeared.

Aid to Ethiopia lagged in the early phases of that famine too. The West was dubious about then president Mengistu Haile Mariam's closeness to the Soviets until BBC and CBC footage, combined with the involvement of rock stars and telethons, shamed governments into increasing the flow of aid.

And not only governments: A farmer from Guelph, Ont., Fred Benson, galvanized by the news from Ethiopia, gave his 107-acre farm to a Mennonite aid agency for the sake of people whose faces he had never seen.

Yet it wasn't much discussed at the time that Mr. Mengistu was arming his troops for a so-called Red Star offensive against the Eritrean rebels with expensive Russian armaments bought with the substance of his starving nation.

With my own eyes, at the time, I saw the astonishing quantities of arms and aircraft he had brought to Eritrea, when I was caught unexpectedly for the better part of the week in a besieged town named Nacfa in the Eritrean highlands.

As an Eritrean minder told me, "He's blowing schools and clinics out of the mouth of his cannon."

At the same time, Mr. Mengistu was putting great emphasis on celebrating the 10th anniversary of his regime, such that Addis Ababa became a Disneyland of Stalinist [referring to Soviet dictator Joseph Stalin] achievement in the midst of a hungering populace.

Few voices were raised to tell us all this, or to tell us about the forced resettlement of millions into unfamiliar country. If we had known it all, would Fred Benson have been as generous? Would there have been a Bob Geldof [Irish performer and political activist]?

For us today, unfortunately, this Horn of Africa famine is another in a string of almost expected events. We expect that the world will get some emergency aid there. We feel as if we have heard the whole story before. Yet it is an utterly fresh and terrifying experience for the people of the "triangle." They have tried every way of survival. They have skimped at meals, have seen what crops they could grow wither and have lost their livestock or tried to sell them in a glutted market. Meanwhile, the grain shortage sends prices up, and even encourages hoarding by merchants, while in their huts farmers face the massive question of whether they should eat next year's seed crop, one of the final acts of familial desperation.

The grain shortage sends prices up, and even encourages hoarding by merchants, while in their huts farmers face the massive question of whether they should eat next year's seed crop.

These starving have looked for eyes of undigested grain in cow manure; they have foraged for wild foods, yehub nuts and berries, in competition with their neighbours. Any family jewellery has been sold. Many starving women probably have been forced to make a Sophie's choice, whether to feed a child likely to die or one not already sick.

And as they slide toward starvation, the devastation of their immune systems will attract assaults by opportunist bacteria. There's no sense of banal repetition in their struggles.

Perhaps we must try a new theorem: to try to get the Somalis and the Ethiopians fed precisely because their governments have not yet created societies in which supply and support are taken for granted.

Aid agencies could be given breaks from endless pie charts about administration costs and aid delivery per donor dollar and stop pretending that they will be permitted to go everywhere they like and to do all the good they can. They should simply invite us into the general struggle to deliver aid as energetically, cleverly and well as the malign circumstances on the desolate ground permit them.

As for the regimes, Mr. Sen's statement glimmers like a tinsel promise, an undeniable though not immediately useful tool, out there in what aid workers call "the field."

But in approaching that dilemma—how to make regimes behave—I have moved far into "wiser-heads-than-mine" territory. And by the time we solved it, there would be millions dead in Africa.

In the United States, the BP Deepwater Horizon Oil Spill Was the Result of Industrial Mistakes

National Commission on the BP Deepwater Horizon Oil Spill and Offshore Drilling

In the following viewpoint, a presidential commission reports its findings on the BP Deepwater Horizon explosion of April 20, 2010. The explosion set off the biggest industrial disaster to ever occur in the Gulf of Mexico. The explosion not only killed many Deepwater Horizon crew members but also caused untold environmental harm to the waters of the Gulf of Mexico, the Louisiana marshlands, and other areas of coastline in the southern United States. The commission concluded that the explosion and subsequent disaster could have been prevented and that its cause was a lack of oversight by both BP and the government.

As you read, consider the following questions:

1. How many crew members were killed in the Deepwater Horizon explosion?
2. What did the commission believe was its first obligation?

"Foreword," *Deep Water: The Gulf Oil Disaster and the Future of Offshore Drilling,* National Commission on the BP Deepwater Horizon Oil Spill and Offshore Drilling, January 2011, pp. vi–x.

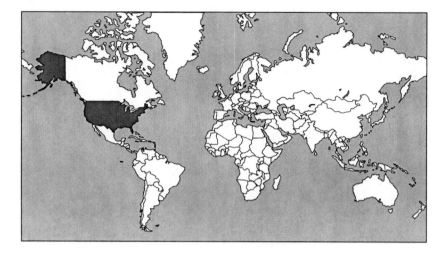

3. Under how many feet of water was the Macondo well drilling? How many feet below the sea floor was the hydrocarbon reservoir?

The explosion that tore through the Deepwater Horizon drilling rig last April 20th [2010], as the rig's crew completed drilling the exploratory Macondo well deep under the waters of the Gulf of Mexico, began a human, economic, and environmental disaster.

Eleven crew members died, and others were seriously injured, as fire engulfed and ultimately destroyed the rig. And, although the nation would not know the full scope of the disaster for weeks, the first of more than four million barrels of oil began gushing uncontrolled into the Gulf—threatening livelihoods, precious habitats, and even a unique way of life. A treasured American landscape, already battered and degraded from years of mismanagement, faced yet another blow as the oil spread and washed ashore. Five years after Hurricane Katrina, the nation was again transfixed, seemingly helpless, as this new tragedy unfolded in the Gulf. The costs from this one industrial accident are not yet fully counted, but it is already clear that the impacts on the region's natural systems and people were enormous, and that economic losses total tens of billions of dollars.

Following the Facts

On May 22, 2010, President Barack Obama announced the creation of the National Commission on the BP [formerly British Petroleum] Deepwater Horizon Oil Spill and Offshore Drilling: an independent, nonpartisan entity, directed to provide a thorough analysis and impartial judgment. The president charged the commission to determine the causes of the disaster, and to improve the country's ability to respond to spills, and to recommend reforms to make offshore energy production safer. And the president said we were to follow the facts wherever they led.

The disaster in the Gulf undermined public faith in the energy industry, government regulators, and even our own capability as a nation to respond to crises.

This report is the result of an intense six-month effort to fulfill the president's charge. From the outset, the commissioners have been determined to learn the essential lessons so expensively revealed in the tragic loss of life on the Deepwater Horizon and the severe damages that ensued. The commission's aim has been to provide the president, policy makers, industry, and the American people a clear, accessible, accurate, and fair account of the largest oil spill in U.S. history: the context for the well itself, how the explosion and spill happened, and how industry and government scrambled to respond to an unprecedented emergency. This was our first obligation: determine what happened, why it happened, and explain it to Americans everywhere.

As a result of our investigation, we conclude:

- The explosive loss of the Macondo well could have been prevented.

- The immediate causes of the Macondo well blowout can be traced to a series of identifiable mistakes made by BP, Halliburton, and Transocean that reveal such systematic failures in risk management that they place in doubt the safety culture of the entire industry.

- Deepwater energy exploration and production, particularly at the frontiers of experience, involve risks for which neither industry nor government has been adequately prepared, but for which they can and must be prepared in the future.

- To assure human safety and environmental protection, regulatory oversight of leasing, energy exploration, and production require reforms even beyond those significant reforms already initiated since the Deepwater Horizon disaster. Fundamental reform will be needed in both the structure of those in charge of regulatory oversight and their internal decision-making process to ensure their political autonomy, technical expertise, and their full consideration of environmental protection concerns.

- Because regulatory oversight alone will not be sufficient to ensure adequate safety, the oil and gas industry will need to take its own, unilateral steps to increase dramatically safety throughout the industry, including self-policing mechanisms that supplement governmental enforcement.

- The technology, laws and regulations, and practices for containing, responding to, and cleaning up spills lag behind the real risks associated with deepwater drilling into large, high-pressure reservoirs of oil and gas located far offshore and thousands of feet below the ocean's surface. Government must close the existing gap and industry must support rather than resist that effort.

- Scientific understanding of environmental conditions in sensitive environments in deep Gulf waters, along the region's coastal habitats, and in areas proposed for more drilling, such as the Arctic, is inadequate. The same is true of the human and natural impacts of oil spills.

We reach these conclusions, and make necessary recommendations, in a constructive spirit: We aim to promote changes that will make American offshore energy exploration and production far safer, today and in the future.

More broadly, the disaster in the Gulf undermined public faith in the energy industry, government regulators, and even our own capability as a nation to respond to crises. It is our hope that a thorough and rigorous accounting, along with focused suggestions for reform, can begin the process of restoring confidence. There is much at stake, not only for the people directly affected in the Gulf region, but for the American people at large. The tremendous resources that exist within our outer continental shelf belong to the nation as a whole. The federal government's authority over the shelf is accordingly plenary, based on its power as both the owner of the resources and in its regulatory capacity as sovereign to protect public health, safety, and welfare. To be allowed to drill on the outer continental shelf is a privilege to be earned, not a private right to be exercised.

Deepwater Drilling Brings Risks

As the board that investigated the loss of the *Columbia* space shuttle noted, "complex systems almost always fail in complex ways." Though it is tempting to single out one crucial misstep or point the finger at one bad actor as the cause of the Deep-

The Extent of Environmental Devastation

On April 22, 2010, fires from an explosion taking place two days earlier, sank the Deepwater Horizon oil rig, located in the Gulf of Mexico about 52 miles (84 kilometers) off the coast of Louisiana. The explosion killed eleven workers and seriously injured seventeen others. The destruction created a massive oil leak from the wellhead located 5,000 feet (1,500 meters) below the surface. Over the next eighty-seven days, the resulting oil spill would become the largest accidental oil spill in history, creating a swath of environmental devastation and death along broad areas of the central and northern Gulf Coast. . . .

By June 2010, the surface slick extended over most of the northern Gulf of Mexico. While the bulk of the spill initially remained at sea, oil began washing into ecologically sensitive marshlands in Louisiana. Extending eastward into Florida waters, the surface slick spotted white-sand beaches vital to local tourist-based economies. Fishing bans extended over more than a quarter of the Gulf of Mexico, resulting in crippling economic hardship and apocalyptic predictions for the future of a Gulf seafood industry integral to the regional economy and deeply entwined with the culture of the region. In Alabama, oil flowed into inland waterways and wetland areas. Deaths of marine mammals, fish, birds, and other wildlife began to spike upwards.

"Gulf Oil Spill," Environmental Encyclopedia. 4th ed.
Ed. K. Lee Lerner, et al. Detroit, MI: Gale, 2011.

water Horizon explosion, any such explanation provides a dangerously incomplete picture of what happened—encouraging the very kind of complacency that led to the accident in the first place. Consistent with the president's request, this report takes an expansive view.

Why was a corporation drilling for oil in mile-deep water 49 miles off the Louisiana coast? To begin, Americans today consume vast amounts of petroleum products—some 18.7 million barrels per day—to fuel our economy. Unlike many other oil-producing countries, the United States relies on private industry—not a state-owned or controlled enterprise—to supply oil, natural gas, and indeed all of our energy resources. This basic trait of our private enterprise system has major implications for how the U.S. government oversees and regulates offshore drilling. It also has advantages in fostering a vigorous and competitive industry, which has led worldwide in advancing the technology of finding and extracting oil and gas.

When a failure happens at such depths, regaining control is a formidable engineering challenge—and the costs of failure, we now know, can be catastrophically high.

Even as land-based oil production extended as far as the northern Alaska frontier, the oil and gas industry began to move offshore. The industry first moved into shallow water and eventually into deep water, where technological advances have opened up vast new reserves of oil and gas in remote areas—in recent decades, much deeper under the water's surface and farther offshore than ever before. The Deepwater Horizon was drilling the Macondo well under 5,000 feet of Gulf water, and then over 13,000 feet under the sea floor to the hydrocarbon reservoir below. It is a complex, even dazzling, enterprise. The remarkable advances that have propelled the move to deepwater drilling merit comparison with exploring outer space. The commission is respectful and admiring of the industry's technological capability.

But drilling in deep water brings new risks, not yet completely addressed by the reviews of where it is safe to drill, what could go wrong, and how to respond if something does go awry. The drilling rigs themselves bristle with potentially dangerous machinery. The deepwater environment is cold, dark, distant, and under high pressures—and the oil and gas reservoirs, when found, exist at even higher pressures (thousands of pounds per square inch), compounding the risks if a well gets out of control. Deepwater Horizon and the Macondo well vividly illustrated all of those very real risks. When a failure happens at such depths, regaining control is a formidable engineering challenge—and the costs of failure, we now know, can be catastrophically high.

Both government and industry failed to anticipate and prevent this catastrophe, and failed again to be prepared to respond to it.

In the years before the Macondo blowout, neither industry nor government adequately addressed these risks. Investments in safety containment, and response equipment and practices failed to keep pace with the rapid move into deepwater drilling. Absent major crises, and given the remarkable financial returns available from deepwater reserves, the business culture succumbed to a false sense of security. The Deepwater Horizon disaster exhibits the costs of a culture of complacency.

The commission examined in great detail what went wrong on the rig itself. Our investigative staff uncovered a wealth of specific information that greatly enhances our understanding of the factors that led to the explosion. . . . There are recurring themes of missed warning signals, failure to share information, and a general lack of appreciation for the risks involved. In the view of the commission, these findings highlight the importance of organizational culture and a consistent commitment to safety by industry, from the highest management levels on down.

Complacency Left the Country Vulnerable

But that complacency affected government as well as industry. The commission has documented the weaknesses and the inadequacies of federal regulation and oversight, and made important recommendations for changes in legal authority, regulations, investments in expertise, and management.

The commission also looked at the effectiveness of the response to the spill. There were remarkable instances of dedication and heroism by individuals involved in the rescue and cleanup. Much was done well—and thanks to a combination of good luck and hard work, the worst-case scenarios did not all come to pass. But it is impossible to argue that the industry or the country was prepared for a disaster of the magnitude of the Deepwater Horizon oil spill. Twenty-one years after the *Exxon Valdez* spill in Alaska, the same blunt response technologies—boom, dispersants, and skimmers—were used, to limited effect. On-the-ground shortcomings in the joint public-private response to an overwhelming spill like that resulting from the blowout of the Macondo well are now evident, and demand public and private investment. So do the weaknesses in local, state, and federal coordination revealed by the emergency. Both government and industry failed to anticipate and prevent this catastrophe, and failed again to be prepared to respond to it.

If we are to make future deepwater drilling safer and more environmentally responsible, we will need to address all these deficiencies together; a piecemeal approach will surely leave us vulnerable to future crises in the communities and natural environments most exposed to offshore energy exploration and production.

A British Analyst Examines the Causes of the 9/11 Disaster in the United States

Peter Bergen

In the following viewpoint, Peter Bergen examines many theories of the causes of the terrorist disaster known as 9/11. The September 11, 2001, disaster was one of the largest in US history, and as Bergen reveals, the underlying factors leading to the catastrophe are complicated and interwoven. Most of the theories in circulation, according to Bergen, are flawed. He offers ten "credible explanations," however, including radicalization of young Muslims, the role of Osama bin Laden, and US foreign policy, among others. Peter Bergen is a British American print journalist and CNN's national security analyst.

As you read, consider the following questions:

1. What are madrasas, according to Bergen?
2. What has been al Qaeda's ultimate goal since at least the mid-1990s, according to Bergen?
3. Who are some of the harshest critics of the 9/11 attacks, according to Bergen?

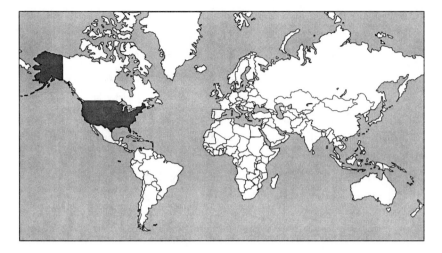

Everyone has a theory about the real causes of 9/11. They range from the nutty (it was the US government) to the plausible but flawed (a response to foreign occupation) to the credible (collateral damage from a clash within Islam).

No event in recent times has produced as many explanations as the 11th September attacks five years ago [in 2001]. Within the space of an hour, [militant Islamist group] al Qaeda inflicted more direct damage on the US than the Soviet Union had done throughout the Cold War, a cataclysm seen by more people than any other event in history. Yet it took only 19 men armed with small knives to destroy the World Trade Center, demolish a wing of the Pentagon and kill 3,000 people. This mismatch has led some—especially in the Muslim world—to seek a deus ex machina to explain what otherwise appears inexplicable. The usual suspects have been assembled on 9/11's grassy knoll: the Jews were behind the attacks; the US government engineered them; the "[Dick] Cheney-[George W.] Bush energy junta" planned them so that they could grab the oil fields of central Asia, and so on.

Osama bin Laden [founder of al Qaeda] himself claims that al Qaeda was solely responsible for 9/11. In 2004, he released a video in which he explained his dealings with lead hijacker Mohammed Atta. After the largest criminal investigation in history, the US government's 9/11 commission also concluded that al Qaeda was solely responsible for the attacks.

The real scandal here is not that the CIA helped to create [Osama] bin Laden during the 1980s, but that the agency had no idea of his significance until sometime in 1996.

Attributing the sole responsibility for 9/11 to al Qaeda then brings us to the larger question: What caused al Qaeda to launch the attacks? Explanations for the attacks can be sorted into two categories—the seemingly plausible but flawed, and the more credible.

Plausible but Flawed Theories

Poverty. Many politicians and commentators see the poverty of the Middle East as a factor. (Some political leaders even argued that the Doha [Development] Round of trade talks [held in Doha, Qatar, in 2001], launched soon after 9/11, were intended partly to quash terrorism.) This claim is not supported by the evidence. Those who attacked on 9/11 were sons of the Middle Eastern middle and upper class, not the dispossessed. Throughout recent history, from the Russian anarchists to the German Baader-Meinhof gang in the 1970s, terrorism has largely been a bourgeois endeavour. Al Qaeda is no different.

Madrasas. A related argument to the poverty canard is that madrasas, religious schools that teach the Koran by rote and sometimes instil a simplistic view of jihad, are breeding grounds for terrorists. Quite the opposite. Madrasa graduates have rarely, if ever, carried out major anti-Western attacks. None of the 9/11 hijackers attended a madrasa and most had been to college, several of them in the West. Bin Laden went to the European-influenced Al-Thager high school and then studied economics at King Abdulaziz University, both in Jeddah [Saudi Arabia].

They hate us because of the freedom-loving people we are. President Bush has been the principal exponent of this view. In 2004 bin Laden responded by asking why, if this were true, had he not attacked freedom-loving Sweden?

The CIA. The notion that bin Laden is a CIA [Central Intelligence Agency] creation, and that the attacks on the Trade Center and Pentagon were "blowback," is a standard analysis among leftists around the world. Indian novelist [Suzanna] Arundhati Roy has written that bin Laden was "among the jihadis who moved to Afghanistan in 1979 when the CIA commenced its operations there. Bin Laden has the distinction of being created by the CIA." This theory is advanced as axiomatic but it has no supporting evidence. The real scandal here is not that the CIA helped to create bin Laden during the 1980s, but that the agency had no idea of his significance until sometime in 1996, when it set up a special unit to track the Saudi exile.

Weak and failing states. It is a staple of international relations theorists that weak and failed states are attractive bases for terrorists and criminals. That the 9/11 attack was first hatched in 1996 as al Qaeda moved its base from a weak state, Sudan, to a failed state, Afghanistan, seems to underline this theory. Certainly al Qaeda thrived under the incompetent rule of the Taliban. However, much of the 9/11 plot took shape in Hamburg [Germany], where most of the pilots and secondary planners of the attack became more radical than they had been while living in their home countries. Although Afghanistan was critical to the rise of al Qaeda, it was the experience that the plotters acquired in the West that made them both more militant and better equipped to carry out the attacks.

There Is No Evidence for Saudi Involvement

Saudi financiers. Little or no hard evidence has been proffered for the claim that Saudi financiers were sponsoring al Qaeda, and the 9/11 report determined that there was no evidence that the money for the attacks came from Saudi Arabia. Moreover, money is not the "oxygen" of terrorism. Terrorism is a cheap form of warfare—the first Trade Center attack in 1993 cost only a few thousand dollars. No amount of money will buy you 19 young men willing to commit suicide in a terrorist operation. According to court documents entered in the trial of the supposed 20th hijacker, Zacarias Moussaoui, the 9/11 operation cost a little over $200,000, a trivial sum considering the damage it inflicted. The pilots who flew the hijacked planes into two of the world's most famous buildings saw what they were doing as an act of worship. Al Qaeda's strength lies not in its material resources, which are small, but in its beliefs.

The Saudis in general. Some commentators have assigned much of the responsibility for the rise of al Qaeda to the Saudis. This is also the contention of many of the families of the victims of the 9/11 attacks, who have signed on to a class action lawsuit against a range of Saudi institutions and individuals. In this view, the Saudi royal family made an unholy alliance with the purist Wahhabi sect and exported Wahhabism in order to shore up its shaky credibility as the custodian of the holy places of Mecca and Medina. The historian Bernard Lewis has observed: "The custodianship of the holy places and the revenues of oil have given worldwide impact to what would otherwise have been an extremist fringe in a marginal country. . . . Imagine that the Ku Klux Klan or some similar group obtains total control of the state of Texas, of its oil and therefore its oil revenues, and having done so, uses this money to establish a network of well-endowed schools and colleges all over Christendom, peddling their own peculiar brand of Christianity."

The Saudi export of Wahhabism did eventually bear disastrous fruit in Afghanistan with the advent of the Taliban, a regime that was recognised and supported by only three countries, including Saudi Arabia, and was influenced by Wahhabist doctrines. However, since at least the mid-1990s, al Qaeda's ultimate goal has been the destruction of the Saudi royal family and so it is a stretch to blame the Saudi state for al Qaeda's recent activities. Moreover, there are millions of Muslims who follow a Wahhabist version of Islam, yet only a very few turn to violence.

The clash of civilisations. Samuel Huntington [American political scientist] famously predicted that clashes between civilisations would replace cold war rivalries, and 9/11 seemed to vindicate his theory. But did it? Most Muslims condemned 9/11, and after the attacks bin Laden's attempt to ignite a clash of civilisations fizzled out. It is rather the US war of choice in Iraq that galvanised anti-Americanism among Muslims.

Other Theories Without Basis

Suicide terrorism, including 9/11, is a response to foreign occupation. In his influential 2005 book *Dying to Win [The Strategic Logic of Suicide Terrorism]*, political scientist Robert Pape examined a series of modern suicide campaigns and concluded that they are driven not by religious zeal but by foreign occupations. Pape pointed out that the secular Tamil Tigers [Liberation Tigers of Tamil Eelam (LTTE) in Sri Lanka] have engaged in one of the most protracted and bloody campaigns of suicide terrorism of the modern era. Pape's theory might explain why 15 of the 9/11 hijackers were Saudis, as there was a substantial US presence in the Saudi kingdom around that time, but it does not explain the other four hijackers, who were Lebanese, Egyptian and Emirati, none of whose countries were occupied by the US.

Moreover, events in Iraq have undermined Pape's contention that foreign occupation is the driving force behind suicide attacks, particularly in the Islamic world. Suicide attackers in Iraq are largely foreigners, and half or more are estimated to be Saudis, while the rest are from other Middle Eastern countries, with a sprinkling of Europeans. Only around 10 per cent of the suicide attacks in Iraq are undertaken by Iraqis. It is not foreign occupation, but rather a globalised culture of martyrdom that is driving suicide attacks in the Muslim world. Indeed, in 2003, US forces in Saudi Arabia—bin Laden's original casus belli [an act or situation justifying war]—were reduced almost to zero, yet bin Laden and his followers continued to advocate attacking the US.

Today political Islam seems to be on the march around the Middle East, and to treat 9/11 as the swansong of militant Islamists seems like wishful thinking.

We are in a clash with a totalitarian ideology, similar to communism. The most serious proponent of this idea is Paul Berman, whose 2003 book *Terror and Liberalism* places "Binladenism" squarely in the tradition of modern millennial totalitarian ideologies such as fascism and communism: "9/11 was an event in the 20th-century mode. It was the clash of ideologies. It was the war between liberalism and the apocalyptic and phantasmagorical movements that have risen up against liberal civilisation ever since the calamities of the First World War." While this idea has some attractions, Binladenism does not pose the existential threat to the West presented by the totalitarian ideologies of the 20th century. And although it is certainly an ideology, it has precious little to do with either communism or Nazism, both of which abolished the very notion of God. Binladenism is not just another totalitarian ideology of the kind which we have seen before. Al Qaeda may use modern technology but it is animated by a 7th-century view of the world that has nothing in common with [Adolf] Hitler or [Joseph] Stalin.

The death rattle of political Islam. Could 9/11 be the last gasp of the radical Islamists? French academic Gilles Kepel has made the point that Islamist states such as Sudan and Taliban-ruled Afghanistan have turned out to be abject failures. In his book *Jihad: The Trail of Political Islam*, published after 9/11, Kepel argued, "in spite of what many commentators contended in its immediate aftermath, the attack on the US was a desperate symbol of the isolation, fragmentation and decline of the Islamist movement, not a sign of its strength." However, Kepel was writing before the US occupation of Iraq, the election of Hamas in Palestine, and the present troubles in Lebanon. Today political Islam seems to be on the march around the Middle East, and to treat 9/11 as the swansong of militant Islamists seems like wishful thinking.

Ten Credible Explanations

None of the following explanations is alone sufficient to explain the attacks, but together they do help us to understand 9/11. They are ranked in ascending order of importance.

10. *Radicalisation caused by the Afghan jihad.* While there is no evidence that the CIA trained or funded bin Laden or his followers, the Afghan war against the Soviet Union nonetheless radicalised a generation of Arab militants. They swapped business cards, gained battlefield experience and came to believe that they had played a big role in the destruction of the Soviet Union. All of these factors would lead to the founding of al Qaeda in 1988, established to take the jihad to other parts of the globe.

9. *A particular reading of Islamic texts.* In the many discussions of the "root causes" of Islamist terrorism, Islam itself is rarely mentioned. But if you were to ask bin Laden, he would say that his war is about the defence of Islam. We need not believe him but we should nevertheless listen to what our enemies are saying. Bin Laden bases justification of his war on a corpus of Muslim beliefs and he finds ammunition in the Ko-

The World Trade Center Disaster: September 11, 2001

On the morning of September 11, 2001, nineteen hijackers seized control of four commercial aircraft that had taken off from East Coast airports, bound for Los Angeles or San Francisco. The hijackers flew one of the planes into the North Tower of the World Trade Center [WTC] in New York City, one into the South Tower, and a third into the Pentagon, the huge military office building in Washington, D.C. The fourth plane's hijackers may have planned to fly it into the Capitol building in Washington, but it crashed near Shanksville, Pennsylvania, after some of the passengers struggled with the hijackers.

The crashes in New York and Washington produced great destruction and created panic and confusion, but worse was to come. The aircraft, loaded with enough fuel to fly across the country, set off very hot fires high in the two stricken office towers of the WTC. Less than an hour after impact, the South Tower collapsed. The North Tower lasted a little more than 100 minutes before it, too, collapsed in an enormous cloud of smoke and debris. Hundreds of firefighters, police officers, and EMTs [emergency medical technicians] had answered the call and were working to rescue people from the burning towers. More than four hundred of them were killed when the towers fell, along with everyone who remained in the doomed structures. Later that day a third, smaller WTC building, which had been struck by part of the falling North Tower, also collapsed.

Rebecca Stefoff, "Deliberate Disaster,"
Forensic and Modern Disasters. *New York:*
Marshall Cavendish Benchmark, 2011, pp. 66–85.

ran to give his war Islamic legitimacy. He often invokes the "sword" verses of the Koran, which urge unprovoked attacks on infidels. Of course, that is a selective reading of the Koran and does not mean Islam is an inherently violent faith, but to believers the book is the word of God.

8. *Decline and stagnation in the Middle East and the "humiliation" of the Islamic world.* Bernard Lewis is the best-known exponent of the idea that the Muslim world is in a crisis largely attributable to centuries of decline, symbolised by the fate of the once powerful Ottoman Empire and its ignominious carve-up by the British and French after the First World War. Lewis also argues that the problems of the Middle East were later compounded by the import of two Western ideas—socialism and secular Arab nationalism—neither of which delivered on their promises of creating prosperous and just societies. The economic and political failures in much of the Muslim world are underlined by statistics such as the fact that the non-oil revenues of all of the gulf states add up to less than the GDP [gross domestic product] of Finland.

Three weeks after 9/11, as the US began launching air strikes against Taliban positions, a video of bin Laden sitting on a rocky outcrop was broadcast on Al Jazeera. On the tape, bin Laden said, "What America is tasting now is something insignificant compared to what we have tasted for scores of years. The Islamic world has been tasting this humiliation and this degradation for 80 years. . . Neither America nor the people who live in it will dream of security before we live in it in Palestine, and not before the infidel armies leave the land of Muhammad." So in his first statement following 9/11, bin Laden emphasised the "humiliation" of the Muslim world and the negative effect of US policies in the Middle East. In this sense, bin Laden seems to agree with Bernard Lewis. Indeed, bin Laden often talks about the "humiliation" suffered by Muslims at the hands of the West. For bin Laden, the 1916 Sykes-Picot agreement that carved up the Ottoman Empire between the French and British has the same resonance that the 1919 Treaty of Versailles did for Hitler. It must be avenged and reversed.

[Osama] bin Laden has made a rational choice to adopt terrorism as a shortcut to transforming the political landscape.

---

7. *The spread of communications technology.* The humiliation felt by some Muslims is amplified by the communications revolution. The umma [also, ummah], the global community of Muslims, is far more aware of conflicts around the Islamic world—and the role of the West in some of those conflicts—than was the case a decade ago. The creation of Al Jazeera in 1996 coincided with bin Laden's first call for a holy war against the US. Since then Arabic satellite channels and jihadist websites have proliferated, sensitising Muslims to the oppression of their co-religionists in Kashmir, Palestine, the Balkans and so on. These grievances have fuelled the spread of al Qaeda's ideology and underpinned the rage of the 9/11 hijackers.

6. *Authoritarian Middle East regimes helped incubate the militants.* Sayyid Qutb, the [Vladimir] Lenin [Communist revolutionary and leader] of the militant jihadist movement, and later Ayman al-Zawahiri, bin Laden's number two, were radicalised by their time in the jails of Cairo. It is no accident that so many members of al Qaeda have been Egyptians and Saudis.

5. *The alienation of Muslim immigrants in the West.* Three of the four 9/11 pilots and two key planners, Ramzi bin al-Shibh and Khalid Sheikh Mohammed, became more militant while living in the West. Perceived discrimination, alienation and homesickness seem to have turned them all in a more radical direction. This is true for other anti-Western terrorists. Swati Pandey [researcher and journalist] and I have examined

the biographies of 79 terrorists responsible for five of the worst recent anti-Western terrorist attacks. We found that one in four of these terrorists had attended colleges in the West.

9/11 was collateral damage in a civil war within the world of political Islam.

---

4. *US foreign policies in the Middle East, in particular its support of Israel.* By bin Laden's own account, this is why al Qaeda is attacking America. His critique has never been cultural; he never mentions Madonna, Hollywood, homosexuality or drugs in his diatribes. US support for Israel, especially the support it gave to Israel's invasion of southern Lebanon in 1982, first triggered bin Laden's anti-Americanism, which during the 1980s took the form of urging a boycott of US goods. He was later outraged by the "defiling" export of 500,000 US troops to Saudi Arabia after Saddam Hussein's invasion of Kuwait in 1990.

Terrorism as a Shortcut

3. *Bin Laden is an astute tactical leader and rational political actor fighting a deeply felt religious war against the West.* Like others before him, bin Laden has made a rational choice to adopt terrorism as a shortcut to transforming the political landscape. It is clear from the 9/11 commission report that bin Laden intervened to make two key decisions that ensured the success of the attacks. The first was to appoint Mohammed Atta to be the lead hijacker; Atta would carry out his responsibilities with grim efficiency. The second was to rein in Khalid Sheikh Mohammed's plans for ten planes to crash into targets in Asia and on the East Coast of America simultaneously. That number of attacks would have been hard to synchronise and might not have succeeded.

2. *9/11 was the collateral damage of a clash within Islam.* The view that 9/11 was the result of a conflict within the

Muslim world was brilliantly articulated in early 2002 by Middle East scholar Michael Scott Doran in a *Foreign Affairs* essay, "Somebody Else's Civil War." Doran argued that bin Laden's followers "consider themselves an island of true believers surrounded by a sea of iniquity and think that the future of religion itself, and therefore the world depends on them and their battle." In particular, Egyptians in al Qaeda, such as Ayman al-Zawahiri, hold this view, inheriting it from Sayyid Qutb, who believed that most of the modern Middle East is living in a state of pagan ignorance. The Egyptian jihadists believed that they should overthrow the "near enemy"— Middle East regimes run by "apostate" rulers. Bin Laden took the next step, urging Zawahiri that the root of the problem was not the "near enemy" but the "far enemy," the US, which propped up the status quo in the Middle East.

Bin Laden's Reasoning

1. *The 9/11 attacks were the fruit of bin Laden's flawed strategic reasoning.* Bin Laden's total dominance of al Qaeda meant the organisation was hostage to his strategic vision. His analysis of US foreign policy was based on the US withdrawal from Lebanon in 1983, after the attack on the barracks that killed 241 American servicemen, and from Somalia in 1993 after 18 US soldiers were killed in Mogadishu. From these retreats, bin Laden concluded that the US was a paper tiger, capable of withstanding only a few strikes before it would withdraw, leaving client regimes in the Middle East vulnerable. But the US response to 9/11 was to destroy the Taliban regime and decimate al Qaeda. Although 9/11 was a tactical success for al Qaeda, it actually threatened the organisation's future.

Some of the harshest critics of the 9/11 attacks have been al Qaeda insiders such as Abd-Al-Halim Adl, who in June 2002 wrote to the 9/11 operational commander, Khalid Sheikh Mohammed, saying: "Today we must completely halt all external actions until we sit down and consider the disaster we caused. The East Asia, Europe, America, Horn of Africa, Yemen, Gulf, and Morocco groups have fallen."

To conclude, 9/11 was collateral damage in a civil war within the world of political Islam. On one side there are those, like bin Laden, who want to install Taliban-style theocracies from Indonesia to Morocco. On the other side there is a silent majority of Muslims who are prepared to deal with the West, who do not see the Taliban as a workable model for modern Islamic states, and who reject violence. Bin Laden adopted a war against "the far enemy" in order to hasten the demise of the "near enemy" regimes in the Middle East. And he used 9/11 to advance that cause. That effort has, so far, largely failed.

Yet bin Laden and his attacks on the US have shaped an ideological movement that will outlive him. Binladenism has drawn tremendous energy from the war in Iraq, and will probably gain further adherents from the conflict in Lebanon. Egyptian leader Hosni Mubarak was prescient when he warned in 2003 that the Iraq war would spawn "100 new bin Ladens." It is that new generation of militants that is bin Laden's legacy.

Periodical and Internet Sources Bibliography

The following articles have been selected to supplement the diverse views presented in this chapter.

Emily Alpert	"Asian Cities Hit Harder by Increasing Disasters, Experts Warn," *Los Angeles Times*, November 13, 2012.
Andy Brice	"The Boom Times: A Guide to Major Chemical Disasters Worldwide," ICIS, October 2, 2008. www.icis.com.
Disasterium	"Information About Disasters," 2011. www.disasterium.com.
Charles D. Ferguson	"Pools of Danger," *Guatemala Times*, April 15, 2011.
Geoscience Australia	"What Is a Bushfire?," July 13, 2011. www.ga.gov.au/hazards/bushfire/bushfire -basics/what.html.
Fiona Harvey	"Floods: A Disaster Waiting to Happen," *Guardian*, February 1, 2013.
Charlotte Hodgman and Mark Omrod	"The Black Death," *BBC History Magazine*, February 2011.
Talea Miller	"Rating Nuclear Accidents and Incidents: Which Were the Worst?," *PBS NewsHour*, March 18, 2011. www.pbs.org.
Campbell Phillips	"Earthquakes: The 10 Biggest in History," *Australian Geographic*, March 14, 2011.
Rob Williams	"Supervolcanoes That Could Destroy Humanity 'May Explode Sooner than Scientists Thought,'" *Independent*, May 31, 2012.

CHAPTER 2

Disasters, Social Issues, and Politics

Poverty Magnifies the Impact of a Disaster

Dan Brook

*In the following viewpoint, Dan Brook argues that the conse-
quences of disaster are human-made, even when the hazard is a
natural event, such as an earthquake. He further asserts that
poverty places people at great risk for the serious consequences of
any natural disaster. The poor are vulnerable to scarcity of resources such as food and water, and since many are malnourished to begin with, any scarcity can be fatal. Brook classifies
poverty as a "chronic disaster," one that is ever present in the
lives of many people of the world. Brook is an instructor of sociology and political science and writes the* Eco-Eating *blog.*

As you read, consider the following questions:

1. What was the magnitude of the December 26, 2004,
   earthquake that caused the tsunami in the Indian
   Ocean?

2. About how many people on Earth have insecure or irregular access to food and clean water?

3. According to Brook, what are some cities at risk of being submerged because of global warming?

D isasters come in many forms.

The 7.0 earthquake that turned the capital of Haiti into a pile of rubble hit on 12 January 2010, causing shocking devastation in an already devastated country. The combination of French colonialism, U.S. military occupation, dictatorial rule, overpopulation, deforestation, capitalist globalization, lack of education, and other factors already made Haiti one of the poorest countries.

On 29 August 2005, Hurricane Katrina slammed into Louisiana, eventually breeching the levees surrounding New Orleans and drowning the city, especially the disproportionately poor and African-American Lower Ninth Ward.

The tsunami that erupted in the Indian Ocean from the massive 9.0 earthquake on 26 December 2004 was incredibly powerful, immensely destructive, and very deadly, perhaps killing a quarter of a million people or more.

I felt—and continue to feel—the pain of these events.

Natural Disasters with Unnatural Consequences

Though these were natural disasters, some of the causes and certainly the consequences were unnatural and not entirely random.

Generally, in Indonesia, the areas with the most destruction, with the possible exception of Banda Aceh, near the epicenter, were the areas where there had been the most economic growth, the most capitalist development, and therefore the most environmental degradation, e.g., primarily tourist infrastructure and shrimp farming that, among other things, destroyed the mangrove forests and coral reefs that serve as rich ecosystems and natural barriers against tidal waves.

My son asked if the people affected by the disaster were (are!) so poor, why didn't we help them before the disaster? A very good question indeed.

Poverty is a chronic tsunami, a constant hurricane, a never-ending earthquake, and the big wave of malnutrition, the fierce winds of hunger, and the planetary rumbling of starvation are ever present. With about a billion people—approximately 1,000,000,000 people!—with insecure and irregular access to enough food and clean water, millions of poor people die each year, tens of thousands of poor people each day, another poor person every few seconds of every day of every year. It boggles my mind and pains my heart. It should inspire us to action.

Food and water are the most basic necessities for all sentient beings, whether people, other animals, or plants. Yet, in most places of the world, food is a commodity for sale, an essential product in search of private profit, a privilege for those who can afford to pay the parasitic price. As basic and existential and material and requisite as it is, food is purposely withheld from those with physical need for those with economic demand regardless of physical condition. Sometimes food is freely given to those in desperate need; mostly it isn't.

Poverty is a chronic tsunami, a constant hurricane, a never-ending earthquake, and the big wave of malnutrition, the fierce winds of hunger, and the planetary rumbling of starvation are ever present.

It is wonderful that we have scientists and others researching and working on treatments and cures for various ailments and diseases. That should certainly continue. But we should also work on the treatments and cures for hunger, dysentery, gastroenteritis, and other very well-known, very easily treated causes of suffering, starvation, and mass death. Treatment involves taking proper care of suffering people; cures imply removing, reforming, or revolutionizing the structures and sys-

Haiti: The Worst-Case Scenario for Disasters

"If you want to put the worst-case scenario together in the Western Hemisphere (for disasters), it's Haiti," said Richard Olson, a professor at Florida International University who directs the Disaster Risk Reduction in the Americas project.

"There's a whole bunch of things working against Haiti. One is the hurricane track. The second is tectonics. Then you have the environmental degradation and the poverty," he said.

Seth Borenstein, "Another View:
Haitian Poverty Heightens Disasters' Impact,"
North Country Times, *January 17, 2010. www.nctimes.com.*

tems that result in such massive yet unnecessary tragedies. It may be complex, but it is not complicated. Food must be an absolute right, not a privilege.

Disasters in Many Forms

Natural disasters come in many forms. Climate change in the form of global warming is a slow tsunami, an ever-present earthquake. We are overheating the earth, cooking the planet, slowly boiling ourselves and many other forms of life to death. We already know what happens when we overheat a car, when we overcook a meal, when our bodies are feverish; we can surmise what will happen if we continue to overheat the earth. It isn't pretty and it will get much uglier.

Tepidly called global warming, some such as Rabbi Arthur Waskow call this type of climate change "global scorching." Regardless, global warming is a global warning. Apparently, reports for and from groups as disparate as the Arctic Climate

Impact Assessment, Greenpeace, the Intergovernmental Panel on Climate Change, Oxfam, the Pentagon, the Union of Concerned Scientists, the World Bank, the World Meteorological Organization, and a vast number of other scientists, political economic analysts, and environmentalists agree. The Pentagon report, for example, states that global warming "should be elevated beyond a scientific debate to a U.S. national security concern," higher even than terrorism, warning of riots and declaring that "future wars will be fought over the issue of survival rather than religion, ideology, or national honor."

I mourn for those killed by the Indian Ocean tsunami, Hurricane Katrina, and the Haitian earthquake. I mourn for those killed each day by the chronic disaster of poverty.

The signs of an overheating Earth are clear and the evidence is rushing in and rising: hotter weather in many places, though colder weather in some places; more frequent and violent storms; mass species extinctions; spread of disease; ecospasms; crop failures; melting glaciers and polar ice caps; earlier springs; rising water temperatures; rising ocean levels; acidification of the oceans; disturbed Atlantic Conveyor [Atlantic Meridional Overturning Circulation, part of the global ocean conveyor belt that helps regulate climate around the North Atlantic] and Gulf Stream systems; submerged islands; loss of coastline; and the threat of submerged cities such as New York, Miami, New Orleans, Bangkok, Dhaka, Tokyo, Shanghai, Sydney, Venice, and many, many other cities. As usual, the poor are being disproportionately affected.

Reducing consumption, reducing waste and emissions, recycling and using recycled goods, using renewable energies instead of fossil fuels such as oil, gas, and coal, protecting and replanting forests, reducing or eliminating meat consumption, and reducing or eliminating smoking are some of the things that should be done. While we should do these things and more, we also need to pressure our governments and the corporations to do much more to be sustainable.

Disasters come in many forms. I mourn for those killed by the Indian Ocean tsunami, Hurricane Katrina, and the Haitian earthquake. I mourn for those killed each day by the chronic disaster of poverty. I mourn for the current and future generations who will suffer from the slow disaster of global warming. We need to stop these disasters before they reach land and affect us with disastrous results. We can do it, but we need to be alert and aware, progressive and proactive, and we need to take immediate action.

Natural Disasters and Women

Lorena Aguilar

In the following viewpoint, Lorena Aguilar discusses statistics demonstrating that disasters impact women differently from men, resulting in comparatively more deaths for women. This tendency is more pronounced, she asserts, in countries where women enjoy fewer rights and have access to fewer resources. She also argues that what is often overlooked is the important role women play in disaster preparedness and recovery. She presses for governments and nongovernmental organizations to work for gender-sensitive disaster risk reduction and the recognition of women's rights. Aguilar is the senior gender advisor for the International Union for Conservation of Nature (IUCN).

As you read, consider the following questions:

1. How many countries were included in the 2007 study conducted by the London School of Economics?

2. What features make women important players of effective risk assessment, early warning, and disaster response, according to Aguilar?

3. What agenda was adopted by the International Conference on Gender and Disaster Risk Reduction in April 2009?

When disasters strike, they do not discriminate. Everyone, without exception in the disaster zone will be affected.

While disasters do not make decisions, people most certainly can and do. Before, during and in the aftermath of disasters, human beings perpetuate social patterns of discrimination, and these entrenched patterns cause certain groups of people to suffer more than others.

Women Are Killed More Often than Men

The differentiated impact of disasters on men and women is primarily caused by the existing gender inequalities manifested. As a 2007 study conducted by London School of Economics shows, taking a sample of up to 141 countries over the period 1981 to 2002, natural disasters and their subsequent impact, on average, kill more women than men or kill women at an earlier age than men related to women's lower socioeconomic status.

Indeed, it is recognized worldwide that people's vulnerability to risks depends to a large extent on the assets they have available. In general, women tend to have more limited access to assets—physical, financial, human, social, and natural capital such as land, credit, decision-making bodies, agricultural inputs, technology, extension and training services which would all enhance their capacity to adapt.

Special attention should therefore be paid to the need to enhance women's capacity to manage risks, with a view to reducing their vulnerability and maintaining or increasing their opportunities for development.

Women Can Help with Risk Reduction

In reality, while women's vulnerability to disasters is often highlighted, their actual and potential roles in disaster risk reduction have often been overlooked. Few existing disaster risk reduction policies and projects recognized the skills and capacities [of] women which could significantly contribute to disaster risk reduction policies and building resilience.

Gender-specific capacities of women deriving from their social roles proved to be beneficial for their whole communities during every stage of the disaster cycle. Women's high level of risk awareness, social networking practices, extensive knowledge of their communities, task in managing natural environmental resources and caring abilities makes them important players of effective risk assessment, early warning, disaster response and recovery actions.

People's vulnerability to risks depends to a large extent on the assets they have available. In general, women tend to have more limited access to assets—physical, financial, human, social, and natural capital.

In Honduras, for example, the village of La Masica was the only community to register no deaths in the wake of the 1998 Hurricane Mitch. Six months earlier, a disaster agency had provided gender-sensitive community education on early warning systems and hazard management. Women took on the abandoned task of continuously monitoring the warning system. As a result, the municipality was able to evacuate the area promptly when the hurricane struck.

Despite the above-mentioned facts, for many years disaster risk reduction has been treated as gender neutral, with disasters seen as physical events requiring only physical prevention and recovery.

As to the latest developments, the Beijing Agenda for Global Action on Gender-Sensitive Disaster Risk Reduction has been adopted at the International Conference on Gender and Disaster Risk Reduction, held from April 20 to 22 this year [2009] in Beijing. This agenda sets nine goals to be achieved before 2015.

Women Hold the Pieces of Family and Community Together

The most urgent tasks of rebuilding daily life in a devastated region . . . usually fall to women. . . .

"Even during conflict, women hold the pieces together and avoid having their families and communities fall apart," [Rania Atalla, executive director of Women for Women International,] says. "Their resilience allows them to feed their children and send them to school . . . to venture out of their homes to ensure their family's survival. These very same skills are highly effective when applied in the effort to rebuild economies in post-conflict countries."

Indira Naidoo,
International Trade Forum, *July 1, 2008.*

Beijing Agenda for Global Action on Gender-Sensitive Disaster Risk Reduction Goals

1. Increase political commitment to gender analysis and gender mainstreaming through enhanced cooperation and collaboration between ministries responsible for disaster risk reduction, climate change, poverty reduction and gender issues, with the participation of civil society;

2. Develop and review national policies, relevant laws, strategies, plans and budgets and take immediate action to mainstream gender into national development policies, planning and programmes;

3. Foster the linkage between disaster risk reduction and climate change adaptation from a gender perspective through policy and administrative measures;

4. Collect gender-specific data and statistics on impact of disasters, carry out gender-sensitive vulnerability, risk and capacity assessments and develop gender-sensitive indicators to monitor and measure progress;

5. Increase awareness of the public and media on the gender-sensitive vulnerabilities and capacities in disasters and gender-specific needs and concerns in disaster risk reduction and management;

6. Support research institutions to study the cost-benefit and efficiency of gender-sensitive policies and pro-grammes in disaster risk reduction, climate change ad-aptation, and poverty reduction;

7. Secure the actual application of disaster risk assessments as part of development policy making and programme formulation to prevent disasters from making the poor even poorer;

8. Improve and mainstream a gender perspective and equal participation between men and women in the coordina-tion of disaster preparedness humanitarian response and recovery through capacity building and training; and

9. Build and enhance the capacities of professional organi-zations, communities and pertinent national and local institutions to enable gender mainstreaming into all de-velopment sectors.

By upholding women's rights we are, in fact, making one of the most crucial preparations associated to disaster risk reduction that any society can make.

Women Can Help Prevent Catastrophes

No amount of human planning, preparedness, or scientific in-vestigation can completely prevent all catastrophes. Neverthe-less, preventing social catastrophes most certainly lies within our collective human capacity. By upholding women's rights we are, in fact, making one of the most crucial preparations associated to disaster risk reduction that any society can make.

VIEWPOINT 3

Women Survivors of the Bhopal Disaster in India Claim Their Rights

Jashodhara Dasgupta

In the following viewpoint, Jashodhara Dasgupta reports on her research concerning the social justice actions of the 1984 Bhopal, India, gas disaster. Though these women are poor, Dasgupta asserts, the event has galvanized them into a cohesive force for social justice. They demand compensation and reparations for the harm done to them by not only Union Carbide, the owner of the factory that released poison gases in their neighborhood, but also the Indian government and other Western companies who pollute and damage their environment. Dasgupta is the coordinator of SAHAYOG, a nongovernmental organization working with women's health and gender equality.

As you read, consider the following questions:

1. How many people have died or been affected by the Bhopal gas disaster after the initial event, according to the viewpoint?

2. How did Rashida Bi's life change in the wake of the disaster, in Dasgupta's view?

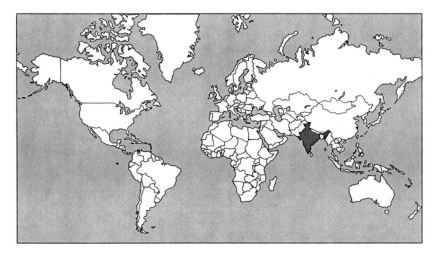

3. With what choice were the women of Bhopal faced immediately after the disaster, according to the viewpoint?

The Bhopal [India] Gas Disaster of December 1984 is perhaps the most horrific industrial disaster anywhere in the world, more so since it was caused by corporate criminal negligence. Just after midnight on 2nd December 1984, an accident in the storage tanks of the Union Carbide (UC) factory at Bhopal caused a massive leakage of a deadly cocktail of MIC (methyl isocyanate), hydrogen cyanide, phosgene and other toxic gases. The white cloud of gases crept out over a sleeping neighbourhood of the poorer quarters of the city near the railway station. In the absence of any warning system, many died in their sleep; others awoke—choking, breathless and blinded. People fled in a stampede, trying to escape or to reach hospitals, some dying on the way. Pregnant women aborted on the streets as the poison seeped into their bodies. Thousands died on that night; the local administration piled bodies into trucks and dumped them into mass graves or threw them into the river. Some recovered consciousness after hitting the cold water; it is unknown if some were buried alive. Since then, tens of thousands more have died: it is estimated that over a hundred and fifty thousand people, mostly an impoverished group of slum dwellers, were affected.

Apart from the loss of family members, some of whom brought home the family income, the survivors had to deal with a lifetime of multiple chronic illnesses related to the gas exposure.

The disaster became global news, since the toxic leak had occurred in a disused factory belonging to a multinational corporation. The chief executive of Union Carbide, Warren Anderson, never faced trial in India. UC handed over the Bhopal factory to the government of Madhya Pradesh with thousands of tons of toxic waste lying around in the open, in violation of its original contract. Research in the 1990s showed severe groundwater contamination due to toxics from the factory. The municipality declared the water from more than 100 hand pumps unfit for drinking. Yet the communities who used the contaminated water were not entitled to health care available for the gas-affected population. In 2001, UC was merged with Dow Chemical [Company] and became the world's largest chemical company. However, Dow refused to accept any responsibility for Bhopal.

The Movement for Claiming Rights

For the poor slum-dwellers of Bhopal, the nightmare had only begun in 1984. Apart from the loss of family members, some of whom brought home the family income, the survivors had to deal with a lifetime of multiple chronic illnesses related to the gas exposure. For many of the men who did physical labour, this meant loss of livelihood. The poisons affected people's eyes, lungs and bloodstream, nerves and muscles, digestive and reproductive systems. Women continue to have spontaneous abortions, stillbirths and menstrual problems.

The toxins were damaging to the body's immune system, yet there was no research information available on the long-term effects of the gases. UC never published information on what the leaking gases actually contained and what were the antidotes that had been researched. Medical treatment remained symptomatic and often expensive; families continued losing even more members to gas exposure–related causes.

Gas-affected families needed immediate relief; later they needed compensation that would be equitably distributed, access to skill-building and alternative livelihood options, employment and social security for the especially vulnerable, and most of all, appropriate and effective medical care. Apart from this, they also demanded information regarding transparent utilization of public resources, and last but not least, justice: that Union Carbide (later Dow Chemical) should acknowledge their criminal negligence in allowing the gas leak to happen and face trial in India for the death of thousands of Indians. But within the maze of complex procedures compounded by state corruption and inefficiency, none of these entitlements could be taken for granted, and survivors were caught up in an endless struggle for a life of dignity. The collusion between the state and the globally powerful perpetrator pitted against an impoverished, ignorant, physically devastated, largely female or minority community of survivors of the most backward sections of a city made this a very unequal contest.

At the professional level, these women demanded their rights as workers; at the public level they were part of the widespread protests against lack of relief, rehabilitation, compensation and justice.

The widespread corruption and state apathy towards the survivors made every step a continuous uphill struggle: in offices, legislative assemblies, municipalities, hospitals, on the streets, and in the courts. The government challenged court orders in favour of the survivors on numerous occasions; the administration refused to implement court orders, or delayed implementation, hoping that the slum-dwellers would eventually give up.

That this prolonged struggle has continued to this day reflects extraordinary tenacity and courage in the face of poverty, crippling ill health, and the disadvantages of class, creed and gender. Initially, the survivors themselves formed mass-based organizations around struggles for livelihoods, compensation, social security and health care. Later, smaller grassroots women's organizations were formed, mostly led by survivors themselves, to continue the demands for their rights. According to one of the leaders, Rashida Bi, 'in the beginning men became leaders, because they were articulate and educated, with experience of being in other campaigns. But . . . the men lost interest very soon. It was the women who persisted . . . in (our organisation), it is the women who take political decisions.'

Women as Activists

The killer gases creeping into the lanes of old Bhopal on the night of 3 December 1984 were to have other unexpected effects—they changed the personal lives of many women beyond recognition. For example, Rashida Bi was a woman from the minority Muslim community without formal education who had been married at 13. She rolled hand-made cigarettes (*beedis*), working at home in *purdah* (veiled). Shabana (name changed) was a young Muslim widow living in Ward 36, in the worst affected area, with her two very small children at the time of the gas leak. Until December 1984, none of them had gone out beyond the lane they lived in. Today, each of these women is a strong activist who is leading or has led the most powerful survivor organizations like the Bhopal Gas Peedit Mahila Udyog [Sangathan] (BGP MUS, the Bhopal Gas Af-

Negligence at the Bhopal Plant

In December 1984, a gas leak of approximately forty metric tons of methyl isocyanate (MIC) from a pesticide plant in Bhopal, India, resulted in as many as 3,000 deaths and injuries to thousands. MIC, an organic chemical used in the production of pesticides, is a volatile liquid that reacts violently with water. MIC is highly toxic to humans and short-term exposure can cause respiratory diseases, if not death, and can seriously affect reproduction. The circumstances and results of what was the industrial accident with the largest death toll in history has been widely used as a case study in engineering design and technology management.

Union Carbide of India, Limited (UCIL), a company controlled by U.S.-based Union Carbide Corporation (UCC), operated the Bhopal plant. UCC provided the basic plant design, supervised its engineering, and defined its operating procedures. Prior to the catastrophe, the plant had been losing money for several years due to weak demand in India for pesticides. This resulted in major personnel reductions, particularly in production and maintenance. At the time of the accident, the plant had been shut down for more than a month for a complete maintenance overhaul. Important safety devices were out of commission and personnel with no MIC training were in supervisory roles. Consequently, when a large amount of water entered an MIC tank due to a mistake during normal maintenance procedure (according to the Indian government version of events), the ensuing reaction caused a large gas leak; defects in the MIC unit and a lack of staff safety training prevented containment.

Deena Murphy-Medley and Joseph Herkert, "Bhopal Case,"
Encyclopedia of Science, Technology, and Ethics. *Ed. Carl Mitcham.*
Detroit, MI: Macmillan Reference USA, 2005.

fected Women's Enterprise Organization) and the Bhopal Gas Peedit Mahila Stationery [Karmchari] Sangh (BGP MSKS, the Bhopal Gas Affected Women Stationery Employees Union), able to challenge the government of India as well as the might of a transnational corporation.

Immediately after the disaster, women from the gas-affected communities were faced with the choice between economic hardship and venturing out to seek a livelihood. Once they stepped out of their homes, they became involved in multiple struggles to claim rights while trying to cling to their livelihood. At the professional level, these women demanded their rights as workers; at the public level they were part of widespread protests against lack of relief, rehabilitation, compensation and justice. At the same time, the women became strong campaigners for environmental issues, since they were worst affected by the gases: Girls and women continued to suffer across generations with menstrual irregularities, miscarriages, malformed babies and poisoned breast milk.

The increasing sense of being 'wronged' appears to have released energies among the outraged population to identify and ally against other forms of social injustice.

The women initially had very little idea what the factory was producing. After the horrific gas disaster they realized it was some kind of toxic substance that could have fatal consequences. Gradually they received information that their exposure to these chemicals would have wide-ranging effects, which would not only last their entire lives but also affect children yet unborn, and their children's children. The toxic wastes dumped outside the factory also turned out to have visible consequences for the surrounding communities: their children, their soil and their water. After the gas leak, the slogan was: 'Union Carbide has committed a crime against us', but later the women began to understand that 'all multinational companies have spread so much poison in our country: they are making us die a slow death, without using any weapons.'

With time they understood that the state was also responsible for inviting a company producing toxic gases and hazardous materials into their city, for allowing them to build a factory so close to human habitation against all norms; and that they would have to fight against the state. When the women understood the politics and economics of multinational corporations involved in the production of pesticides, they became determined to resist the entry of such corporations into the country. Women activists protested locally, nationally, in courtrooms and in corporate offices at the international level. Women survivors stormed the Mumbai Dow office brandishing brooms and chanting the slogan 'jhaadu maro Dow ko' (brush off Dow with a broom). Women survivors travelled to Dow offices across the world, meeting Dow executives in Europe and US, handing over a broom to each of them, saying 'Clean up our soil and water, for our mothers' milk is contaminated and we will give birth to monsters eighteen years later.'

The increasing sense of being 'wronged' appears to have released energies among the outraged population to identify and ally against other forms of social injustice occurring elsewhere in India. At the same time, they were constantly combating notions of what was culturally appropriate for them as women in the personal sphere. They were dealing simultaneously with their own personal crises in life and relationships. This complex intertwining of the personal and the political in the process of claiming women's rights enabled them to move far beyond their ascribed gender roles.

Natural Disasters Can Cause Political Instability and Conflict

Elizabeth Ferris

In the following viewpoint, Elizabeth Ferris discusses the intersection of natural disasters, conflict, and human rights. She argues that a natural hazard exacerbated by poverty can become a catastrophic disaster. In such cases, governments often topple and chaos ensues, adding to the suffering of those in the region. Sometimes such chaos results in long-term conflict and civil war. In addition, she asserts, countries already experiencing conflict are much less able to respond adequately to any disaster. Ferris is a senior fellow in the Foreign Policy Studies Program at the Brookings Institution.

As you read, consider the following questions:

1. Why, according to Ferris, is it important to incorporate a human rights perspective into natural disaster response?

2. What are some examples of places where natural disasters occurred while the country was in conflict?

3. What examples does Ferris offer of countries whose governments failed largely because of discontent over the way the disaster response was handled?

Responding to natural disasters has traditionally been seen as a compassionate response to people in need. While compassion remains at the core of humanitarian action, relief agencies are increasingly conscious of the fact that assistance is rarely neutral and that their actions can have long-term consequences, as evidenced by the 2004 tsunamis in Asia, Hurricane Katrina in 2005 and the earthquake this year [2010] in Haiti. . . . I'd like to explore some of the connections between sudden-onset natural disasters, conflicts, and human rights. In particular, I argue that incorporating a human rights perspective into natural disaster response is important not only because it affirms the rights and dignity of vulnerable people, but also because it can prevent conflicts in the aftermath of disasters.

A natural disaster is defined by the UN [United Nations] as: "the consequences of events triggered by natural hazards that overwhelm local response capacity and seriously affect the social and economic development of a region." In other words, a cyclone that strikes only an uninhabited island is not a natural disaster. Nor is it a natural disaster when municipal authorities are able to respond effectively to flooding in their community. There are questions about just how 'natural' are natural disasters. For example, the devastating toll on Haiti of 4 hurricanes in 2008 was obviously the result of the storms themselves, but certainly exacerbated by the long-term deforestation in that country and inadequate public response. In fact, in that year, deadly hurricanes hit both Haiti and Cuba, but while 800 people died in Haiti, only four fatalities in Cuba were reported.

The Relationship Between Poverty and Disasters

The evidence is clear that poverty is an important factor in understanding the effects of natural disasters. On 10 December 1988, an earthquake registering 6.9 on the Richter scale hit Armenia, killing some 55,000 people and leaving 500,000 homeless. Less than a year later, in October 1989, an even stronger earthquake, 7.1 on the Richter scale, hit San Francisco, California, killing 62 and leaving 12,000 homeless. Within countries, it is almost always the poor and marginalized who are disproportionately affected by natural disasters. They tend to live in less safe environments and in less safe shelter. Shoddily constructed slums are more vulnerable to earthquakes, landslides and flooding than the homes where the rich are more likely to live. Thus in the recent earthquake in Haiti, the homes of the country's elite were located in neighborhoods which were less impacted by the tremors and their homes were more likely to withstand the shocks than those of poorer neighborhoods.

Natural disasters exacerbate existing gender inequalities and preexisting vulnerabilities. The majority of those who die in natural disasters are women. Women also tend to have less access to essential resources for preparedness, mitigation, and rehabilitation. Assistance can often be discriminatory in impact even if not intended to be so. Government policies can reinforce social divisions.

The evidence is clear that poverty is an important factor in understanding the effects of natural disasters.

The frequency and severity of sudden-onset natural disasters is increasing. Presently there are about 400 natural disasters per year, affecting 200 million people. This is double the number reported 20 years ago. In particular hydrometeorological events are increasing—most likely as the result of climate change. Of the 200 million people whose lives are affected by natural disasters, around 36 million were forced to leave their homes in 2008 and are considered to be internally displaced persons. Unlike those displaced by conflict, this displacement is usually temporary and almost always occurs within the borders of the country. However, as our own Hurricane Katrina demonstrates, displacement can last a long time. It is estimated that about a quarter of those displaced by Hurricane Katrina have not returned.

Natural Disasters and Conflict

There are several ways of exploring this relationship: What is the cumulative effect of natural disasters and conflict on people's lives? Do natural disasters contribute to conflict? Does the response to natural disasters help resolve conflicts? Or make them worse?

There are cases where natural disasters occur in places where conflict has already disrupted the lives of people, for example, the Philippines, Iraq, Somalia, Kenya, Colombia, and Haiti. Because the definition of a natural disaster is linked to the society's response capacity, state and social structures which are weakened by conflicts are less likely to be able to respond to the effects of a natural hazard, making it more likely that a natural disaster will result. For example, the Somali government is extremely weak (controlling only a few blocks of the capital city) as a result of long-standing conflict and thus unable to respond to either the drought or flooding which has occurred in its country. If there were no conflict in Somalia, it is more likely that both the state and community institutions would be better able to cope with the natural hazards, perhaps avoiding disasters all together.

Although the situations vary, the occurrence of a natural disaster in an area affected by ongoing conflict can lead to:

- increased misery for people whose lives have already been disrupted by conflict. For example, in the Philippines camps for people displaced by conflict in Mindanao were flooded in 2008, reportedly undermining their coping skills.

- further displacement as when people displaced by conflict are forced to move yet again because of the disaster. In the case of the Mindanao floods, some of the conflict IDPs [internally displaced people] were forced to move again as a result of the flooding. Or following the tsunami in Sri Lanka, some of those displaced by the conflict were displaced again by the storm surge.

- increased hardship on communities hosting the displaced. Thus in Somalia, rural areas hard-hit by flooding in 2009 were already having difficulties growing sufficient food for their communities. The arrival of Somalis displaced by the fighting in Mogadishu increased the strain on these communities. The majority of recent IDPs from Mogadishu went to the nearby Afgoye corridor—making it the "highest density of internally displaced persons in the world—over half a million IDPs along a stretch of 15 kilometers of road."

- more difficulties for relief agencies in accessing affected communities. This is particularly the case for countries in governments that are unwilling to extend access to humanitarian actors. For example, after the 1990 earthquake in Gilan Province in Iran which measured 7.7 on the Richter scale, killed 50,000 people and decimated entire villages, the government initially insisted that the country would handle the crisis on its own and turned away international assistance. By the time the government was willing to enlist assistance from abroad, a significant proportion of the affected had reportedly died from otherwise preventable deaths. A similar initial rejection of international aid by the government of Burma/Myanmar following the May 2008 Cyclone Nargis complicated the relief effort.

It seems to make intuitive sense to conclude that conflicts worsen the impact of natural disasters by weakening state, community and individual capacity to respond.

There are surprisingly few long-term empirical studies on the relationship between conflict and natural disasters. [Researchers Philip] Nel and [Marjolein] Righarts looked at data for 187 countries and other political entities for the period 1950 to 2000 and found that rapid-onset natural disasters significantly increase the risk of violent civil conflict both in the short and medium term, specifically in low- and middle-income countries that have high inequality, mixed political regimes (which are neither fully autocratic or democratic), and sluggish economic growth. Similarly, [R.S.] Olson and [A.C.] Drury found that the more developed a country, the less likely a natural disaster is to have political consequences. . . .

It seems to make intuitive sense to conclude that conflicts worsen the impact of natural disasters by weakening state, community and individual capacity to respond.

In other words, it seems that particularly for developing countries with weak governments, a natural disaster can cause political instability. Indeed, in countries such as Guatemala (1976 earthquake) and Nicaragua (1976 earthquake), governments have fallen largely because of popular discontent over the way the disaster response was organized. Indeed, the poor response of the West Pakistan government to the 1970 typhoon in East Pakistan was a principal reason for the ensuing war which resulted in Bangladeshi independence the following year.

Tsunamis and Conflict

One of the most interesting comparisons of the relationship between conflict and natural disasters is the effect of the 2004 tsunamis on conflicts in Sri Lanka and Aceh, Indonesia. At the time the tsunamis struck, both countries were mired in pro-tracted conflicts. In Aceh, the response to the tsunami seems to have contributed to the resolution of a long-term simmer-ing conflict between Gerakan Aceh Merdeka (GAM) and the government. In contrast, the response to the tsunami in Sri Lanka seems to have exacerbated tensions between the Tamil Tigers (the Liberation Tigers of Tamil Eelam (LTTE)) and the government of Sri Lanka.

What made the difference? As is usual in these situations, there are many factors which are responsible for both the con-flict and for its resolution. Several researchers have made the point that these two cases were at different 'stages' of conflict and that the tsunami (and the response to the disaster) had different impacts on the warring parties. [Field researcher Pe-ter] Bauman [and his colleagues] argue that in the 30-year-old Indonesia/Aceh conflict, both sides had come to realize that a military solution was unviable and were looking for a political solution, but lacked an exit strategy. Both the government and the insurgents were seriously affected by the tsunami. The government lacked the capacity to rebuild Aceh without inter-national support and was forced to allow international actors into the region—which had previously been largely denied be-cause of the conflict. The international presence provided a sense of security to the population and coupled with both strong international support and committed political leader-ship, peace negotiations were restarted. In August 2005, a memorandum of understanding was signed in which the In-donesian government recognized the right of Aceh to "special autonomy," a solution short of the secession which had been demanded earlier. This agreement ended nearly 30 years of conflict which had caused 15,000 deaths and displaced up to 150,000–250,000 people.

In comparison, when the tsunami struck Sri Lanka, the peace process was similarly stalled, the LTTE held a strong po-sition and the tsunami itself affected the Tamil and Sinhalese communities differently. At the time, the majority of the 390,000 conflict-induced IDPs lived in the north and east and were Tamil. But the majority—though by no means all—of those affected by the tsunami were Sinhalese living in the south. An estimated 457,000 Sri Lankans were displaced by the tsunami. While there was a lot of talk in Sri Lanka about joining together to respond to the victims of the tsunami, in fact, there were tensions from the beginning as both sides sought to use the occasion—and the relief—to strengthen their own positions. . . .

It seems that particularly for developing countries with weak governments, a natural disaster can cause political instability.

One of the lessons of the tsunami is an affirmation of [development economist] Mary Anderson's classic argument that humanitarian assistance can either mitigate or accelerate conflicts. This is also a major factor in conflict-induced displacement as humanitarian assistance can be diverted to support armed groups and actually prolong the conflict.

Natural Disasters and Human Rights

It was the 2004 tsunami which brought the issue of human rights and natural disaster response to the fore of the international agenda. In part this was because of the sheer magnitude of the disaster and the scale of the response. Unlike most natural disasters, the response to the tsunamis was well funded. With sufficient funding, relief agencies were able to develop ambitious programs and generally did not need to coordinate their efforts with others. At its worst, this led to competition between agencies for beneficiaries and awareness of the discriminatory impact of assistance. While such discrimination has likely been a feature in most disaster relief efforts, the sheer presence of hundreds of NGOs [nongovernmental organizations], bilateral aid agencies, and international organizations made it more apparent to observers. The fact that relief agencies were generally well resourced also made it possible for them to devote more resources to monitoring and evaluation—which also highlighted not only inequitable patterns of assistance, but a range of protection issues.

In response to the tsunami, the Representative of the [UN] Secretary-General on the Human Rights of Internally Displaced Persons, Walter Kälin, developed *Operational Guidelines on Human Rights and Natural Disasters* which were adopted by the Inter-Agency Standing Committee [IASC] in 2006 and focus on what humanitarian actors should do to implement a rights-based approach to humanitarian action in the context of natural disasters. They provide concrete guidance on how to ensure that the rights of those affected by disasters are respected, are currently being revised on the basis of feedback from the field, and serve as a basis for a number of training and awareness-raising initiatives. They are based on the conviction that human rights are the legal underpinning of all humanitarian work related to natural disasters and to most humanitarian work with victims of internal conflicts.

These guidelines emphasize that:

- Persons affected by natural disasters should enjoy the same rights and freedoms under human rights law as others in their country and not be discriminated against.

- States have the primary duty and responsibility to provide assistance to persons affected by natural disasters and to protect their human rights.

- Organizations providing protection and assistance accept that human rights underpin all humanitarian action.

- All communities affected by the disaster should be entitled to easily accessible information concerning the nature of the disaster they're facing, possible mitigation measures that can be taken, early warning information, and information about ongoing humanitarian assistance.

The problems that are often encountered by persons affected by natural disasters include: unequal access to assistance; discrimination in aid provision; enforced relocation; sexual and gender-based violence; loss of documentation; recruitment of children into fighting forces; unsafe or involuntary return or resettlement; and issues of property restitution. These are similar to the problems experienced by those displaced or otherwise affected by conflicts.

Protecting Human Rights

Although there is considerable discussion within the human rights community about prioritizing certain rights, it is generally accepted that the first priority is to protect life, personal security, and the physical integrity and dignity of affected populations by:

- Carrying out evacuations and relocations when necessary in order to protect life.

- Protecting populations against the negative impacts of natural hazards.

- Protecting populations against violence, including gender-based violence.

- Providing security in camps when these are necessary.

- Protecting people against anti-personnel land mines and other explosive devices.

A second category of rights are those related to basic necessities of life, including:

- Access to goods and services and humanitarian assistance.

- Provision of adequate food, and sanitation, shelter, clothing and essential health services.

Protection of other economic, social and cultural rights, including:

- Education

- Property and possessions

- Housing

- Livelihood and work

Finally, other civil and political rights need to be protected:

- Documentation

- Freedom of movement and right to return

- Family life and missing or dead relatives

- Expression, assembly and association, and religion

- Electoral rights

This offers concrete guidance to those responding to natural disasters—whether governments, international organizations, or nongovernmental organizations. For example, in the immediate aftermath of a flood, governments are often not able to provide necessary educational facilities for affected children. This can (and must) come later, once the children are protected against violence and have access to the basic necessities of life. Similarly, the right to documentation is a crucial issue for many affected by emergencies, but affected communities have a more urgent need for sufficient food and water.

Even with the best of intentions by all concerned, it is sometimes not possible to ensure that the rights of all those affected by an emergency are fully and immediately respected. For example, access to affected populations is often difficult, those responsible for responding to disasters may themselves be affected, groups who are already socially vulnerable are usually the most affected by disasters and the logistical demands of ensuring that needed assistance items are in the right place and are delivered may be significant. Resources are almost always limited in the initial phase of disaster response. However, in preparing for disasters, governments and relief agencies can and should carry out their planning in such a way as to ensure that human rights are respected. And with the passage of time, it is usually more feasible for disaster response to incorporate an explicitly human rights focus.

Adopting a human rights–based response to those affected by natural disasters is a concrete way to ensure that natural disasters do not exacerbate existing or provoke new conflicts.

More than treaties and checklists, planning for emergency response requires adoption of a human rights perspective or mind-set. This means that responders should constantly be asking themselves questions such as: "Who are the vulnerable groups in this community and how do our plans ensure that they are protected and assisted?" "Even as we're working to supply water to this community, is someone else working on the next phase of providing education and protecting the property of those who have left?" "How will our actions affect the rights of those who are not living in camps?" Developing a human rights mind-set requires not only an understanding of international and national standards, but also a commitment to ensuring that the inherent dignity and basic human rights of all people are upheld.

Adopting a human rights–based response to those affected by natural disasters is a concrete way to ensure that natural disasters do not exacerbate existing or provoke new conflicts.

Politics Negatively Affected Cyclone Nargis Disaster Relief in Myanmar

Donald M. Seekins

In the following viewpoint, Donald M. Seekins reports on the humanitarian crisis caused by Cyclone Nargis when it slammed into Myanmar (also known as Burma). The storm caused flooding in the densely populated Irrawaddy Delta and the largest city of Rangoon (Yangon). Although the United Nations, foreign governments, and many aid organizations were quick to respond to the disaster, Myanmar's military regime blocked foreign aid for political purposes. As a result, many more people died or were seriously injured. Seekins is a professor of Southeast Asian studies at Meio University.

As you read, consider the following questions:

1. What two reasons does Seekins give for the likelihood that fatalities would rise after the storm?
2. Why did Buddhist monks demonstrate in Myanmar in September 2007, according to the viewpoint?
3. What did the *Los Angeles Times* report on May 10, 2008, concerning food reaching cyclone victims?

Donald M. Seekins, "The Social, Political and Humanitarian Impact of Burma's Cyclone Nargis," *Asia-Pacific Journal: Japan Focus*, May 26, 2008. Reproduced by permission.

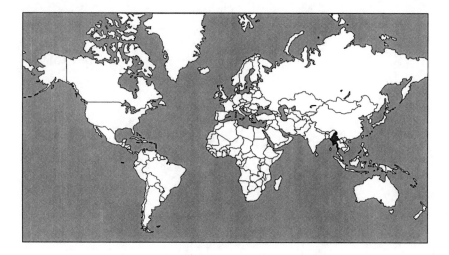

This [viewpoint] provides background information and analysis concerning the humanitarian crisis caused by Cyclone Nargis when it passed through the densely populated Irrawaddy Delta and Burma's largest city Rangoon (Yangon) on May 2–3, 2008. One of the largest natural disasters in recent history, it caused the death of as many as 130,000 people (the official figure on May 16 was 78,000) and resulted in between one and two million people losing their homes and property.

Fatalities are likely to rise both because of the extremely unsanitary conditions in the disaster area, and the slowness of the State Peace and Development Council (SPDC), the Burmese military government, in getting assistance where it is most needed.

Burma's Government Impedes Relief

In the days following the storm, the SPDC placed major obstacles in the way of the rapid distribution of relief goods and services by the United Nations [UN], foreign governments, international nongovernmental organizations and local volunteer groups—a situation that has continued despite warnings from aid experts that a second, man-made disaster—the systematic neglect of people gravely weakened by thirst, hunger and disease and many more fatalities—is on the verge of occurring.

On May 10, the SPDC carried out a referendum on a new military-sponsored constitution, though the vote was postponed to May 24 in the townships most affected by the cyclone. Observers wondered why the referendum was considered so important by the SPDC, given the scale of the natural disaster and the need to commit resources immediately to its alleviation. Resources inside the country that could have been used for relief in the Irrawaddy Delta and Rangoon were in fact used to make sure that the referendum was carried out smoothly.

The military junta was originally willing to accept medicine, food, temporary shelters and other relief goods from foreign parties, but did not wish to have foreign aid workers inside the country distributing these goods or performing other services such as medical care and public health education. This is because the generals fear that a large number of foreigners would be politically destabilizing and they would be able to report to the outside world on conditions inside the country. As a result, the very small number of foreign journalists in the country (the authorities have been attempting to locate and deport them) and Burmese witnesses say that the government's relief efforts have been grossly inadequate, given the scale of the catastrophe. Observers generally agree that only about a quarter of the worst affected population in the disaster area has received aid. As of this writing (May 26, 2008), it is unclear whether Senior General Than Shwe's promise to United Nations Secretary-General Ban Ki-moon on May 23 that "all" aid supplies and aid experts from foreign civilian sources would be accepted represents a genuine change of heart or is merely a tactic to hold the international community at bay while the military regime seeks to reassert full control over the Irrawaddy Delta.

The humanitarian disaster caused by Cyclone Nargis is likely to have widespread social, economic and political implications for a country where the military regime's concern for human security as well as human rights has always been minimal. Although the SPDC has expanded armed forces manpower more than 200 percent since 1988 and has allocated a large part of its budget to purchase weapons from abroad and build a new capital, Naypyidaw, 335 kilometers [208 miles] north of Rangoon, it has invested little in health or social welfare. Indeed, many observers claim that social and educational services were actually better under the pre-1988 socialist regime of General Ne Win than under the post-socialist military regime. As a result, Burma is one of the poorest countries in Southeast Asia, outranked in terms of human security and social welfare even by such (former) "basket cases" as Cambodia and East Timor.

The very small number of foreign journalists in the country . . . and Burmese witnesses say that the government's relief efforts have been grossly inadequate, given the scale of the catastrophe.

Despite heavy repression, popular unrest has periodically flared up, most recently in September 2007 when Buddhist monks and ordinary citizens demonstrated en masse in Rangoon and other towns over steep price hikes for fuel and the SPDC's brutal treatment of protesters, especially Buddhist monks. The "Saffron Revolution" (so called because of the color of Buddhist monks' robes) was the largest popular movement in Burma since the pro-democracy demonstrations of 1988. . . .

International Response

Once information about Cyclone Nargis's devastation reached the outside world, plans were made for an effective international response. Donors could draw on the recent experience of the 2004 Indian Ocean earthquake and tsunami to deal with a situation that was similar in many if not most respects. The United Nations called for US$187 million in funds for Burma relief. The French, British and US navies had ships located near the storm-struck delta from which aid materials could be brought quickly by helicopter.

On the ground, people were mystified by the SPDC government's passive response to the disaster. Few troops or members of the Union Solidarity and Development Association (USDA), a pro-government "grassroots" organization, were evident on the streets of Rangoon or in the delta; local residents and Buddhist monks were doing most of the recovery work, including removal of fallen trees and utility poles and the provision of temporary shelters. One group especially prominent in relief efforts both in Rangoon and the delta has been the Free Funeral Service Society, a civil society group organized in recent years by Kyaw Thu, a well-known actor and dissident, to provide decent burial for people whose survivors are too poor to afford it.

One woman in Rangoon complained: "where are all those uniformed people who are always ready to beat monks and civilians? They should come out in full force and help clean up the area and restore electricity." She was referring to the "Saffron Revolution" protests of September 2007, when troops, riot police and paramilitary groups were quickly and efficiently mustered to crush dissent, causing (according to opposition sources) as many as two hundred deaths. Similar expressions of frustration were heard throughout the disaster area in the days that followed. On May 11, Japanese broadcast network NHK televised a feature in which a Burmese doctor interviewed in a makeshift clinic stated that no relief measures had been taken by the authorities, and injured or sick people had received absolutely no assistance. According to the INGO [international nongovernmental organization] Médecins sans

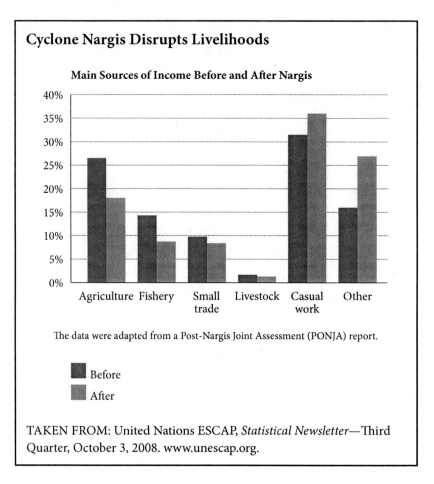

Cyclone Nargis Disrupts Livelihoods

Main Sources of Income Before and After Nargis

The data were adapted from a Post-Nargis Joint Assessment (PONJA) report.

■ Before
■ After

TAKEN FROM: United Nations ESCAP, *Statistical Newsletter*—Third Quarter, October 3, 2008. www.unescap.org.

Frontières [Doctors Without Borders], "More than one week after the disaster, despite the sending of three cargo planes and some positive signals, it has been very difficult to provide highly needed supplies for the heavily affected population in Myanmar... In the areas we have been we haven't seen any aid being delivered so far, so the amount that has reached people in the areas where we are has been minimal."

Military Government Is Slow to Respond

Although the SPDC affirmed that it was ready to receive foreign assistance, it became evident in the days following the cyclone that while it was willing to accept supplies, it did not want a large number of foreign experts inside the country, including persons monitoring the distribution of relief goods or involved in long-term post-disaster development projects. Only a trickle of aid came in, mostly by air to Rangoon's Mingaladon airport. Some of it was confiscated and placed in storage by the authorities, but later released. Aid workers were subjected to long visa application processes at the embassy in Bangkok and elsewhere, planes waited at airports in neighboring countries for permission to deliver their supplies and relief personnel already in the country were given little or no assistance by the government in getting to the worst hit areas, where, as mentioned, as many as 2.5 million people were at risk a week after the storm.

The humanitarian disaster caused by Cyclone Nargis is likely to have widespread social, economic and political implications for a country where the military regime's concern for human security . . . has always been minimal.

The junta's initial slow reaction to the disaster is perhaps understandable: Burmese army and police have been trained exclusively in imposing internal order, not disaster relief. Moreover, there has been no catastrophe like Cyclone Nargis in living memory in Burma (in contrast to Bangladesh, where major cyclones have frequently caused huge losses of life). But in the aftermath of the cyclone, the SPDC's behavior has seemed at times unbelievably callous. The May 10 referendum on the new constitution went ahead as planned, except in areas worst hit by the cyclone where the voting was held on May 24; the state media devoted more attention to the vote than to the natural disaster, including a telecast in which young ladies sung cheerful songs urging the people to cast their ballots "with sincerity" for the sake of the nation. SPDC Chairman Senior General Than Shwe, who kept an extremely low profile in his new capital of Naypyidaw in the days immediately following the disaster, was shown on state television casting his "yes" vote on May 10 for the new basic law along with his wife Daw Khaing Khaing.

Moreover, the *Los Angeles Times* reported on May 10 that while little food or fresh water was reaching the cyclone victims, rice was being exported from the Thilawa container port south of Rangoon to Bangladesh, apparently in an effort to generate foreign exchange while world rice prices are high. Such rice exports are not the responsibility of the private sector, but of a state corporation under the direct control of the military. People interviewed in the area said that they had received small amounts of "rotting" rice from the government, while officials kept supplies of instant noodles for themselves. On May 11, the *International Herald Tribune* reported that Burmese rice was also being shipped from Rangoon to Malaysia and Singapore.

On the ground, people were mystified by the SPDC [State Peace and Development Council] government's passive response to the disaster.

By late May, spurred by the urgings of UN Secretary-General Ban [Ki-moon], who met with SPDC top general Than Shwe on May 23, a larger volume of aid has flowed in and the government has promised to allow foreign aid experts to work without restrictions in the affected areas. Yet the SPDC's overall response to the disaster seems to be motivated by the principle that "politics is in command"—to borrow [former Chinese ruler] Mao Zedong's well-known phrase. This is true in three ways. First, the military regime has made the country's unity, independence and self-reliance a central theme in its propaganda, as reflected in the "Three Main National Causes" adopted after the SLORC [State Law and Order Restoration Council] takeover in September 1988: "non-disintegration of the Union," "non-disintegration of national solidarity" and "perpetuation of national sovereignty"; and in another group of slogans, "People's Desire," which include "oppose those relying on external elements, acting as stooges, holding negative views" and "crush all internal and external destructive elements as the common enemy." For a regime so proud of its self-sufficiency to admit that it is helpless in the face of the cyclone disaster would be—for Than Shwe and his fellow generals—a terrible loss of face, even though the alternative—many more deaths and ever greater popular hatred of the SPDC—would undermine their legitimacy in the longer run.

The Possibility of Destabilization

Secondly, apart from considerations of face and prestige, the arrival of hundreds if not thousands of foreign relief workers in the delta and Rangoon would have great potential for destabilizing an already tense political situation, especially in light of the large anti-government protests of September 2007. It would show ordinary people more vividly than ever how poor and undeveloped Burma has become under military rule, in comparison not only with Western countries but Burma's Asian neighbors (for example, Indonesia has promised substantial aid). Space might be opened up in which people could organize themselves more effectively against the regime with tacit if not open international approval. In the generals' eyes, a foreign presence in the disaster area on the scale of the 2004 Indian Ocean earthquake seems to be more unthinkable than accepting death tolls far higher than the May 16 official figure of around 78,000 or even the UN estimate of 130,000.

Thirdly, the SPDC can use aid donated by the United Nations and foreign countries to deepen the chasm between "Us" (the military and civilian supporters of the regime, such as the USDA) and "Them" (practically everyone else) in Burmese society. By using political rather than needs-based criteria to divert relief supplies to its supporters, the junta hopes it can solidify its grip on power even while the population at large regards it with increasing hatred and contempt.

This reflects a highly ironic development: SPDC apologists routinely accuse the old British colonial regime of dividing the Burmese people against themselves (especially ethnic minorities such as the Karens who served in the colonial army and police against the ethnic majority Burmans) while setting themselves up as an elite caste who became rich from the sale of the country's natural resources. However, in the evolving political system that will be more firmly established with the almost unanimous (and highly manipulated) approval of a new constitution on May 10th and 24th, the Burman-dominated army has isolated itself not only from frontier area ethnic minorities such as the Karens, Shans and Kachins, but also from the largely Burman population in the central part of the country. While ordinary soldiers are often very poor, higher ranks enjoy their own schools and colleges, hospitals and clinics, stores, golf courses, comfortable living spaces and above all business connections that allow them to enjoy a standard of living far superior to that of civilians. Most military personnel live in self-contained cantonments not unlike those of the British colonial era.

In the generals' eyes, a foreign presence in the disaster area ... seems to be more unthinkable than accepting death tolls far higher than the ... official figure of around 78,000 or even the UN estimate of 130,000.

To preserve its power base in an environment of growing scarcity (following the cyclone), the SPDC has to provide the 400,000 members of the armed forces and their families (a total of about two million people) and pro-regime groups such as the USDA, which was established in the early 1990s by Senior General Than Shwe, and the Swan Arr Shin ("Masters of Force"), a paramilitary group of more recent origin, with basic necessities, even while making little or no effort to make them available to the general population. This may explain reports that food obtained from abroad such as high energy biscuits is being placed in army storehouses while the people are being given poor-quality rice and other inferior foodstuffs.

Suppressing Civilian Dissent

The USDA and Swan Arr Shin ("Masters of Force" in Burmese) have played an increasingly important role in suppressing civilian dissent, not only during the September 2007 "Saffron Revolution" but in the "Black Friday" incident of May 30, 2003, when toughs associated with the USDA attacked Daw Aung San Suu Kyi and her supporters in Sagaing Division in Upper Burma, killing as many as 70 or 80 people. There is speculation that the USDA might be transformed under the new constitution into a "mass" political party ... that would function as the military regime's main pillar of "popular" support in the new constitutional order.

In late 2005, Than Shwe ordered the removal of the nation's capital from crowded and unrest-plagued Rangoon to a new city, Naypyidaw, in the central part of the country. The new capital site is relatively isolated and thinly populated, an ideal location from which to control Burma's population in a largely coercive manner, a further decisive step in the isolation of the military elite from the society as a whole. Observers commented cynically that Senior General Than Shwe had been warned by his personal astrologer to move the capital, lest he and his fellow generals be overthrown; but the major factor in the capital relocation seems to have been the desire of the junta to insulate itself from popular unrest in Rangoon and other major cities.

Haiti's Earthquake Disaster Is Exacerbated by Politics and Poverty

Andrew Apter

In the following viewpoint, Andrew Apter argues that all disasters, and particularly the Haiti earthquake, are "simultaneously social and political." He asserts that Haiti's poverty and unstable government make it particularly vulnerable to the terrible consequences of natural hazards. In addition, the fact that most of the country's capital is held in the hands of very few people makes it unstable. Apter, however, sees a possible positive outcome of the earthquake: Because both the rich and the poor suffered death and destruction in the disaster, the earthquake may be a leveling force in the country. Apter is a professor of history and anthropology at University of California, Los Angeles.

As you read, consider the following questions:

1. What is the "lavalas movement" and who was its leader, according to the viewpoint?
2. What was the result of the 1991–1994 embargo of Haiti, according to the viewpoint?
3. With whom did Hillary Clinton meet in Port-au-Prince on January 16, 2010?

Andrew Apter, "Haiti's Earthquake and the Politics of Distribution," Social Science Research Council, January 26, 2010. Reproduced by permission.

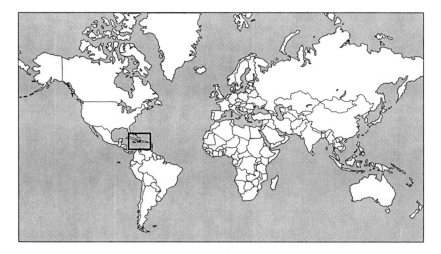

If all natural disasters are simultaneously social and political, Haiti's current earthquake crisis drives the point home with tragic force. As we are reminded of Haiti's dire poverty and misery—the poorest nation in the Western Hemisphere, literacy rates below fifty percent, deteriorated infrastructure, inadequate health services, and the egregious inequality between rich and poor—we can only wonder where Haiti lies on the Richter scale of sociopolitical cataclysms. The combined natural and political debacle has proven to be a double indemnity as Haiti's hapless leadership flounders in the chaos, scarcely visible or audible in its desperate appeals for international assistance. And even with help and resources at the gates, Haiti remains paralyzed by its limited capabilities; unable to free survivors from rubble, disinter the dead, distribute supplies, or sustain basic transport and communications systems.

A Self-Destructive Cycle

It is too easy to blame the victims, and that is not my intention here despite the serious culpability of Haiti's political class. Haiti's chronic poverty and political violence, careening between oppressive dictatorships, states of emergency, bloody elections and military coups are rooted in the logic of a particular system, historically determined to be sure, subject to change and variation, but locked into a self-destructive cycle that seems impossible to break. If ever there was a leader up to the task it was Jean-Bertrand Aristide, whose lavalas movement [Fanmi Lavalas, a political party claiming "growth with equity" as its goal] "from the parish of the poor" built its momentum from a truly popular base.

Haiti's inability to manage international relief is not merely a logistical problem, but a political problem with a long economic history.

But as Aristide would discover, the system he set out to transform got the better part of him, culminating in political assassinations, nepotistic plundering and domination by decree. Not that the "system" acted on its own, since Haiti is a nexus of regional circuits and global forces including transnational capital controlled by elites, Haiti's "tenth department" living abroad, the manifold forms of US occupation (including the detention and deportation of "illegal" immigrants, the war on drugs, even the rise and fall of Aristide himself) and fluctuating flows of international aid. However, what I would like to bring out in this brief rumination is the structural logic of the earthquake disaster—not of geological fault lines and tectonic plates, but of elite control over the means of distribution. Haiti's inability to manage international relief is not merely a logistical problem, but a political problem with a long economic history.

Today, Haiti is paradoxically a "low wage" and "high cost" producer because if labor is cheap, doing business is expensive. Like many entrepôt [a place where goods are stored] countries that impose duties on commodities flowing through their gates, Haiti's gross domestic product is largely extractive, siphoning off cuts by licensing agents when money and commodities cross boundaries and trade hands. What does Haiti actually produce and export? Major agricultural exports include mangos and coffee, whereas manufacturing exports include textiles and apparel. These industries are concentrated in the hands of an oligopoly [a market dominated by a small number of players] that preys on foreign capital through tightly controlled channels of distribution. If Haiti is the poorest nation in the Western Hemisphere, it has the highest port fees in the Western Hemisphere, discouraging outside capital investment. Furthermore, the profits that do accrue within Haiti remain with the elites, who indulge in luxury spending and shopping sprees abroad while supporting a patronage system that keeps them protected within gated communities. The "trickle down" of such wealth to the masses is minimal, maintaining drivers, gardeners, bodyguards and domestic servants on the merest margins of subsistence, while leaving the rest to fend for themselves. Thanks to the 1991–4 embargo which devastated Haiti's agricultural sector, and the dumping of US agricultural surpluses tied to humanitarian aid, Haiti must import flour and rice to meet its subsistence needs. Moreover, rural poverty has led to massive deforestation as desperate Haitians cut trees to make charcoal, further eroding the agricultural base by destroying the ecosystem. To be sure, the informal sector of recycled castoffs, religious goods and services, and narco-trafficking keeps families alive and makes some people rich, as has the growing flow of remittances from Haitians living abroad. The bustling commerce of local markets keeps people afloat on precariously narrow profit margins. But here again, distribution trumps production in the political economy of daily survival.

The Earthquake as a Social Leveler

One of the ironies of Haiti's earthquake is the leveling effect it has had on the nation, bringing together rich and poor within a common community of death and destruction. When the elite's control of the channels of distribution collapsed into rubble, the state virtually withered away, having lost its raison d'être [reason for being] as a mechanism of extraction and domination. But if in this chaos lies a window of opportunity to rebuild Haiti along more viable lines, and thus break the cycle of crises generated by the politics of distribution, the moment will quickly pass. On January 16, 2010, [US Secretary of State] Hillary Clinton flew into Port-au-Prince on a military plane to meet with president René Préval, and announced: "We are here at the invitation of your government to help you. As President [Barack] Obama has said, we will be here today, tomorrow and for the time ahead." The reporter of this meeting noted that "the sound of helicopters and airplanes coming and going was heard in the background," as if setting the stage for the next US occupation and the restoration of the status quo ante.

One of the ironies of Haiti's earthquake is the leveling effect it has had on the nation, bringing together rich and poor within a common community of death and destruction.

As Haiti rebuilds with international assistance, all partners in the effort should work toward a productive and progressive transformation, one that decreases Haiti's dependence on imports and handouts, builds a sustainable infrastructure within Port-au-Prince and throughout the nation, restores agricultural productivity, and rebuilds the environment. A tall order to be sure, but necessary for Haiti to break the vicious cycle of political, economic and ecological devastation. Clearly the solution must be collective, inclusive, multinational and multipronged, with Haitians intimately involved in the process. I would recommend a green agenda, starting with the construction of a solar power grid and solar cookers that would bring clean energy to all communities and households, improve self-reliance, offset the need for charcoal, and put Haiti at the forefront of sustainable "third world" development. As the money for rebuilding comes in, the politics of distribution count more than ever before.

Periodical and Internet Sources Bibliography

The following articles have been selected to supplement the diverse views presented in this chapter.

Sunil Dang	"Of Rail Accidents and Natural Disasters," *Day After* (India), October 1, 2012. www.dayafterindia.com.
Tricia Holly Davis	"Iran: Empowering Women in Disaster Situations," United Nations Office for Disaster Risk Reduction, February 4, 2013. www.unisdr.org.
Jesse Dykstra	"Climate Change, Natural Disasters and Human Vulnerability," *New Zealand Herald*, January 7, 2011.
Economist	"Always with Us: Poverty," February 11, 2012.
Dan Farber	"Did Hurricane Sandy Save Obamacare? How Disaster Relief Justifies the Welfare State," *Washington Monthly*, January–February 2013.
Dylan Grey	"Aid and Politics After Cyclone Nargis," New Mandala, May 3, 2009. http://asiapacific.anu.edu.
Evan Osnos	"Boss Rail: The Disaster That Exposed the Underside of the Boom," *New Yorker*, October 22, 2012.
Pilar Pezoa	"The Impact of Catastrophe," *Women's Health Journal*, January–June 2010.
Jeffrey D. Sachs	"Famine and Hope in the Horn of Africa," Project Syndicate, July 31, 2011. www.project-syndicate.org.
Sara Sorcher	"Syria's Chemical Weapons: A Perfect Storm," *National Journal*, July 13, 2012.

Disaster Preparedness

Better Global Preparedness for Natural Disasters Would Save Lives

Bill McGuire, as told to Robin McKie

In the following viewpoint, British journalist Robin McKie interviews University College London professor of geophysical and climate hazards Bill McGuire. McGuire argues that a global clearinghouse of all the details of all disasters occurring worldwide would be a valuable tool for disaster management. Governments could access the database for warnings and analyses of hazards, allowing them to better prepare and prevent disasters. McGuire further asserts that the rising population of the world as well as climate change makes such a technology investment more crucial than ever.

As you read, consider the following questions:

1. According to the viewpoint, what will happen at high latitudes as the climate warms?
2. What event happened on Boxing Day in 2004, according to McGuire?
3. What two reasons does McGuire give for people's increased vulnerability to natural hazards in the future?

Bill McGuire, as told to Robin McKie, "My Bright Idea: Global Databanks Could Warn of Natural Disasters," *The Observer*, May 8, 2011, p. 24. Reproduced by permission.

Devastating natural disasters have killed close to a million people and caused billions of £ [British pounds] of damage in the past few years. Despite its sophisticated technology, humanity remains hugely vulnerable to earthquakes, hurricanes, volcanic eruptions and other calamities. The danger is only likely to increase, say geologists and weather experts. Earth's swelling numbers are forcing more and more people to live in geological and meteorological danger zones. As a result, death tolls are destined to rise.

In addition, human impact on the climate, which is warming relentlessly as more and more carbon dioxide is pumped into the atmosphere from cars, factories and power stations, will also worsen the problem. At higher latitudes, melting glaciers and ice sheets will modify the pressures acting on tectonic plates and volcanoes, potentially provoking more earthquakes and eruptions, while rising sea levels will leave many regions more vulnerable to hurricanes and storms.

Our Planet Needs Help

Our planet needs help, badly, and Bill McGuire, professor of geophysical and climate hazards at University College London, believes he has a solution. We need a global clearinghouse in which details of all major natural threats are stored, evaluated and updated. All governments and other stakeholders can access the repository to obtain specific information on the hazards that threaten them, whether storm, quake, volcanic blast or tsunami, he says.

[*Robin McKie:*] *There have been several recent catastrophes, including earthquakes in Haiti, Chile, New Zealand and Japan. Would the global clearinghouse you propose have helped lower their death tolls?*

[Bill McGuire:] Not in every case. The earthquake in Japan, which triggered the tsunami on 11 March [2011], arose from a geological fault that was not thought to be capable of releasing such devastating energies. The Christchurch earthquake in February, which killed more than 180 people, was set off by a fault that geologists did not even know about.

However, there have been many other examples in which dangers had been raised by geologists but which were not then passed on to governments or emergency managers, or at least not acted upon. Consider the Haitian earthquake of January 2010. It caused more than 250,000 deaths and up to $14bn [billion] of damage. Yet a scientific paper had been published a year earlier that contained a quite specific warning that the area was at high risk of suffering a major earthquake. Similarly, the dangers of the Chilean earthquake of February 2010, which caused around 500 deaths, had been highlighted in advance in another scientific paper.

We need a global clearinghouse in which details of all major natural threats are stored, evaluated and updated.

On a personal level, I warned the Ministry of Defence several years ago of the dangers to aviation that could be posed by a major Icelandic volcanic eruption. The chaos that reigned when Eyjafjallajökull erupted last year [2010] and our air transport was paralysed suggests that the warning had little influence on government preparedness.

Can you pinpoint any places that are at risk of disaster in the near future?

Yes. There are several. The Boxing Day tsunami of 2004 in the Indian Ocean was triggered by a massive release of energy on a geological fault. However, there is one section along that fault which has still not released its energy. That could be triggered very soon. When it does, it is likely to cause a major earthquake and a tsunami with the potential to swamp the city of Padang, in Sumatra, and its population of more than 800,000 people.

On the other side of the world, it is known that the Caribbean experiences a major earthquake—that is, measuring more

Information Technology Helps in Disaster Management

The challenge of disaster management is reducing the harm disasters cause to society, the economy, and the lives of individuals and communities. That task requires disaster managers to reduce uncertainty, to calculate and compare costs and benefits, and to manage resources, often on a much larger scale and at a much faster pace than are supported by methods and means for solving ordinary problems. IT [information technology] provides capabilities that can help people grasp the dynamic realities of a disaster more clearly and help them formulate better decisions more quickly. And IT can help keep better track of the myriad details involved in all phases of disaster management. . . .

IT has as-yet-unrealized potential to improve how communities, the nation, and the global community handle disasters.

Ramesh R. Rao, Jon Eisenberg, and Ted Schmitt, eds.,
Improving Disaster Management: The Role of IT in Mitigation,
Preparedness, Response, and Recovery. *Washington, DC:*
National Academies Press, 2007, p. 1.

than 8.0 on the Richter scale—sometimes accompanied by a tsunami, every 50 years on average. There has not been one for more than 60 years, however (last year's Haiti quake measured 7.0). So the level of concern is growing.

It is one thing saying such risks exist, but how can ordinary people deal with them?

That is a harder question to answer, and the key is better warning systems. To have these, however, you need to know the nature of the threats, which is where the repository comes in. There is movement, but it is slow. The Caribbean tsunami threat is now taken seriously enough that a warning system is planned. Without it, a big submarine quake in the future could see a tsunami crashing without any warning on to the shores of islands distant from the quake epicentre.

Even when and if a warning system becomes operational, there is still some way to go before a message that a wave is on its way can be transmitted in good time to the guy who runs that bar on the beach and to the people who are drinking there.

But effective warning systems need good, reliable information about the hazard they are intended to warn against, which is where the repository comes in. The idea is not new and was recommended by a committee, of which I was a member, established by [British Prime Minister] Tony Blair after the 2004 tsunami. Despite the interest of the UN [United Nations], there has been no further progress.

Do you believe we will face increased risks of such events in the future?

Yes. The projected two billion rise in the world's population will inevitably mean that far more people are vulnerable, particularly in the great coastal megacities of the developing world. In addition, we know from studies of periods of abrupt environmental change from the past—for example, after the end of the last ice age—that ongoing climate change is likely to drive more geological hazards. Already the loss of ice in Alaska is driving more earthquakes, while rising temperatures in mountainous regions are provoking a rise in the numbers of massive landslides.

Effective warning systems need good, reliable information about the hazard they are intended to warn against.

Future ice loss and bending of the crust due to rising sea levels have the potential ultimately to raise levels of both earthquake and volcanic activity. In short, we may well see a response from the solid earth to climate change and we need to be prepared for that.

Counting the Cost of Calamities

The Economist

In the following viewpoint, London-based newsmagazine the Economist *asserts that death rates from natural disasters are falling and that the number of natural disasters in the world is not increasing. The viewpoint argues, however, that the costs associated with disasters are rising rapidly and show no sign of slowing. The Dutch, therefore, have devised a way to protect their country from disasters and the expenses associated with them. Rather than simply building higher levees, they are engaging in a proactive flood management policy that includes polder removal and making cities more flood resistant. The system could help other countries protect their citizens and their assets from losses, asserts the* Economist.

As you read, consider the following questions:

1. How many deaths did the Bangladeshi cyclones cause in 1970?

2. According to the World Bank, what percentage of humanitarian aid is now spent on responding to disasters and what percentage is spent on preventative measures?

3. What did the Dutch government have to persuade farmers to do in the Noordwaard polder, according to the viewpoint?

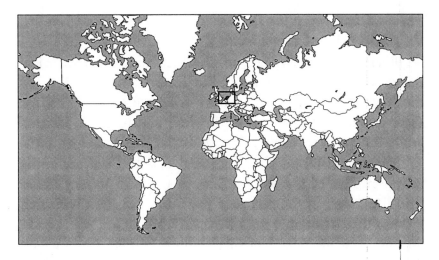

*D*eath *rates from natural disasters are falling; and fears that they have become more common are misplaced. But their economic cost is rising relentlessly.*

The world's industrial supply chains were only just recovering from Japan's earthquake and tsunami in March [2011] when a natural disaster severed them again in October. An unusually heavy monsoon season swelled rivers and overwhelmed reservoirs in northern Thailand. The floodwaters eventually reached Bangkok, causing a political crisis as residents fought over whose neighbourhoods would flood. But before that the economic toll was being felt farther north in Ayutthaya province, a manufacturing hub. The waters overwhelmed the six-metre-high [about 18 feet] dykes around the Rojana industrial estate, one of several such parks that host local- and foreign-owned factories.

Honda's workers rescued newly built cars by driving them to nearby bridges and hills. The factory ended up under two metres (about 6 feet) of water and is still closed. Honda was hardly alone: The industrial estates that radiate out from Bangkok are home to many links in the world's automotive and technology supply chains. Western Digital, a maker of computer disk drives which has 60% of its production in

Thailand, had two of its factories closed by the floods, sending the global price of drives soaring.

Thailand is no stranger to floods. Europeans once called Bangkok the "Venice of Asia". But rarely have they done so much economic damage. October's deluge cost $40 billion, the most expensive disaster in the country's history. J.P. Morgan estimates that it set back global industrial production by 2.5%.

Such multi-billion-dollar natural disasters are becoming common. Five of the ten costliest, in terms of money rather than lives, were in the past four years. Munich Re, a reinsurer, reckons their economic costs were $378 billion last year, breaking the previous record of $262 billion in 2005 (in constant 2011 dollars). Besides the Japanese and Thai calamities, New Zealand suffered an earthquake, Australia and China floods, and America a cocktail of hurricanes, tornadoes, wildfires and floods. Barack Obama issued a record 99 "major disaster declarations" in 2011.

Acts of God, or Man?

Although deadly quakes are rarely blamed on human activity, it is fashionable to blame weather-related disasters on global warming. It does seem plausible: Warm air worsens droughts and lets tropical air hold more moisture, the fuel for cyclones (weather formations that include hurricanes and typhoons). However, a recent study by the Intergovernmental Panel on Climate Change, which represents the consensus among thousands of scientists, expressed little confidence in any link between climate change and the frequency of tropical cyclones.

The world has succeeded in making natural disasters less deadly, through better early-warning systems for tsunamis, better public information about evacuation plans, tougher building codes in quake-prone areas and encouragement for homeowners to adopt simple precautions such as installing tornado-proof rooms in their homes. Annual death tolls are heavily influenced by outliers, such as Haiti's earthquake in

2010 (which killed more than 200,000) or the Bangladeshi cyclones in 1970 (300,000). But, adjusted for the earth's growing population, the trend in death rates is clearly downward.

However, even if natural disasters may be no more common and no more likely to kill people than before, there is no doubt that their economic cost is rising. This is because a growing share of the world's population and economic activity is being concentrated in disaster-prone places: on tropical coasts and river deltas, near forests and along earthquake fault lines.

Thailand is an example of this. Since its last serious floods, in 1983 and 1995, the country's export-oriented industrial base has grown rapidly in the provinces around Bangkok and farther north along the Chao Phraya River. Ammar Siamwalla, a Thai economist, notes that the central plain where many industrial estates now sit was once heavily cultivated for rice precisely because it floods regularly. Although dykes (called levees in America) protect these estates and central Bangkok, they may raise water levels, and thus the risk of flooding, elsewhere.

Wildfires, which destroyed thousands of homes in Texas in 2011 and in Australia in 2009, were more destructive than hitherto because, as populations have grown, new housing has been built in wooded areas. Throughout America's west and south-west, encroaching suburbia has put pressure on forest managers to suppress fires as quickly as possible. Yet repeated fire suppression allows forests to accumulate more fuel which can lead to more intense and devastating fires later on.

Australia's "Black Saturday" bushfires ([not] pictured above), which killed 173 people and destroyed 2,298 homes in 2009, were said to be the country's worst natural disaster. But a study by Ryan Crompton of Macquarie University and others found that 25% of the destroyed buildings were in bushland and 60% were within ten metres of it, and thus exposed to the threat of fire. The study concluded that if previous fires had occurred with people living so close to the bush as today, a 1939 outbreak of wildfires would have been the deadliest while Black Saturday's would rank second, and only fourth by number of buildings destroyed.

In Harm's Way

America's coasts may be a microcosm of where the world is headed. Florida's population has grown from 2.8m in 1950 to 19m now. Howard Kunreuther and Erwann Michel-Kerjan, disaster experts at the Wharton business school in Pennsylvania, reckon there are now nearly $10 trillion of insured and hurricane-prone assets along the coast from Maine round the Florida peninsula to Texas. Roger Pielke of the University of Colorado at Boulder reckons that the Great Miami Hurricane of 1926, which cost $1 billion in 2011 dollars, would cause $188 billion of damage now.

Whether the economic toll of disasters is rising faster than global GDP is unclear, since a wealthier world naturally has more wealth at risk. Still, the incidence of spectacular, multi-billion-dollar catastrophes seems certain to rise. A 2007 study led by the OECD reckoned that by 2070, seven of the ten greatest urban concentrations of economic assets (buildings, infrastructure and the like) that are exposed to coastal flooding will be in the developing world; none was in 2005. In that time, assets exposed to such flooding will rise from 5% of world GDP to 9%. A World Bank study led by Apurva Sanghi estimated that between 2000 and 2050 the city populations exposed to tropical cyclones or earthquakes will more than double, rising from 11% to 16% of the world's population.

Development by its nature also aggravates risks. As cities encroach on coasts, wetlands and rivers, natural barriers such as mangrove swamps and sand dunes are obliterated and artificial ones—dykes and sea walls—are erected to keep the water out. The result is to put more people and property in harm's way if those barriers fail. After the Second World War

Japan embarked on a vigorous programme of building sea-walls and dykes to protect its cities against storm surges and tsunamis. That in turn encouraged cities' growth and industrialisation, but for the same reason exposed them to damage if a tsunami overwhelmed their defences, as it did in March.

As cities on river deltas extract groundwater for industry, drinking and sanitation, the ground subsides, putting it further below sea level and thus requiring even higher dykes. Since 1980 Jakarta's population has more than doubled, to 24m, and should reach 35m by 2020. Land that once absorbed overflow from the city's 13 rivers has been developed, and is now subsiding; 40% of the city is now below sea level.

Perverse Incentives

People originally settled in river deltas precisely because regular flooding made the land so fertile. Those cities have continued to grow because of the natural economic advantages such concentrations of human talent hold for modernising societies. Even when poor people moving to cities know they are increasing their risk of dying in a mudslide or flood, that is more than compensated for by the better-paying work available in cities. And in rich countries, coasts are gaining population simply because people like living near water.

Perverse incentives are also at work. In America, homeowners on floodplains must have flood insurance to get a federally backed mortgage. But federal insurance is often subsidised and many people are either exempt from the rule or live in places where flood risks have not been properly mapped. Some do not buy disaster insurance, assuming they can count on federal aid if their home is destroyed. Once the government declares a disaster, it pays 75-100% of the response costs. Presidents have found it increasingly hard to turn down pleas from local leaders for assistance, especially in election years. Matt Mayer of the Heritage Foundation, a conservative think tank, says the government routinely takes charge of local disasters that should be well within a state's capability. The result is that state disaster-management atrophies and disaster funding ends up subsidising disaster-prone places like Florida at the expense of safer states like Ohio.

As a consequence of these skewed incentives, people routinely rebuild in areas that have already been devastated. Bob Meyer of the Wharton School gives the example of Pass Christian, a resort town in Mississippi, where an apartment complex was destroyed by Hurricane Camille in 1969, killing 21 people who had taken refuge inside. A shopping centre and condominiums were later built in the same area, only to be wiped out by Hurricane Katrina in 2005, since when more new condominiums have gone up nearby.

This is not all because of incentives. As Mr Meyer says, people have a tendency not to price rare, unpredictable events into their decisions, even if these may have catastrophic consequences. Leo "Chipper" McDermott, the mayor of Pass Christian, notes that more than three decades elapsed between Camille and Katrina. "Life is a chance. And let me tell you something else: water sells."

If human nature cannot be changed, government policy can be. That might mean spending more on preventing disaster so as to cut its costs. Roughly 20% of humanitarian aid is now spent responding to disasters, whereas a paltry (but rising) 0.7% is spent on preventive measures taken to mitigate their possible consequences, according to the World Bank.

A Dutch Rethink

The Netherlands, whose existence has long been at the mercy of nature, may be at the forefront of rethinking how to cope with it. Some 60% of the country is either under sea level or at risk of regular flooding from the North Sea or the Rhine, Meuse and Scheldt Rivers and their tributaries. In 1953, a combination of a high spring tide and severe storm over the North Sea overwhelmed dykes, flooding 9% of its farmland

and killing 1,800 people. The country responded with a decades-long programme of "delta works" to guard estuaries from storm surges, while raising and strengthening dykes.

Even if natural disasters may be no more common and no more likely to kill people than before, there is no doubt that their economic cost is rising.

The success of those defences has, perversely, made the consequences of failure even greater, says Piet Dircke of Arcadis, a Dutch engineering firm specialising in water management. Protected by the delta works and dykes, the land stretching from Amsterdam to Rotterdam has heavily industrialised and now provides most of the country's output. "The northern and southern parts of the Netherlands are far more safe but are economically less attractive. People are moving to the western part of Holland because it's where the economy grows."

In 1993 and again in 1995 heavy river flooding inundated the countryside and nearly rose above dykes in population centres, forcing the evacuation of more than 250,000 people. Katrina was the final wake-up call, making the Dutch face up to both the unreliability of forecasts of once-in-a-century events and the impossibility of their repeating the American feat of evacuating a million people.

The country's philosophy of flood control has as a result pivoted from building ever higher dykes to instead making its cities and countryside more resilient to floodwaters. In 2007 it launched its €2.3 billion [about 3 billion] "Room for the River" project. At 39 locations along the Meuse, Rhine, IJssel and Waal Rivers, dykes are being moved inland, riverbeds deepened and fields now occupied by farms and households deliberately exposed to floods. The Dutch invented the word "polder" centuries ago to describe dry land created by enclosing floodplains (or shallow waters) with dykes. They are now

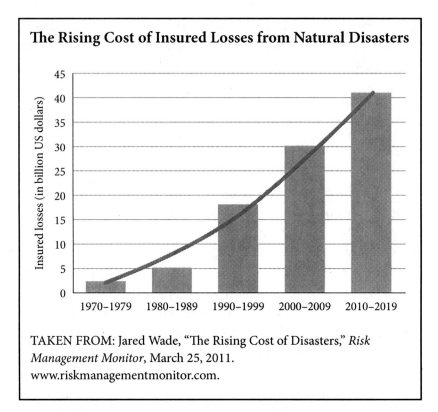

The Rising Cost of Insured Losses from Natural Disasters

TAKEN FROM: Jared Wade, "The Rising Cost of Disasters," *Risk Management Monitor*, March 25, 2011. www.riskmanagementmonitor.com.

"depolderising", removing or lowering the surrounding dykes and turning land back into floodplains. The Rhine's maximum flow without causing disaster will be raised from 15,000 cubic metres [about 4 million gallons] a second to 16,000 [about 4.22 million gallons] and, eventually, 18,000 [about 4.75 million gallons].

The [Netherlands'] philosophy of flood control has as a result pivoted from building ever higher dykes to instead making its cities and countryside more resilient to floodwaters.

The Noordwaard polder south-east of Rotterdam was floodplain until 1973, when the delta works made it suitable for cattle and vegetables. It is now being turned back into floodplain to absorb floodwaters that might otherwise inundate cities upstream. To do so, the government had to persuade 18 farmers to move or have their farmhouses raised. Wim de Wit, who raises 75 cattle on the farm his father started in 1979, chose the latter. Near his farmhouse, earthmoving equipment is building a mound, or "terp," on which a new one will sit, safe from the periodic floods that will follow. It will not be pleasant, Mr de Wit acknowledges, "but it's only once every 25 years." And if he loses any crops or cattle to floods, the government will compensate him.

The Dutch are building an industry of promoting their water-management philosophy around the world. Deltares, a research institute, recommends that the Thai government emulate Room for the River by moving dykes farther back where possible, limiting floodplain development and unifying water management so that safety is no longer subservient to irrigation and electricity generation.

But the Dutch approach has limits. For one thing it is costly. Farmers were paid market value to leave the polders. To do this in a more densely populated city or industrial area would be prohibitively expensive. In America and China, the government has long had the right to breach dykes and periodically inundate occupied land to relieve extreme flooding. Jaap Kwadijk of Deltares notes that the Dutch government has previously rejected doing the same thing. If a flood comes along that exceeds even the very high designed capacity of the dykes, "we don't have a plan B."

If cities cannot be moved, they must, like the polder farms, be made more resilient to disaster. Rather than rely on dykes to keep water out, Rotterdam is also trying to mitigate the consequences if water comes in. A 10,000-cubic-metre [2.6 million gallons] tank was built into a new car park, big enough to catch roughly 25% of the water from a once-in-century flood. A public plaza has been designed to turn into wading pools when it fills with rainwater.

In the city's harbour sits a floating pavilion shaped like three halved footballs built on huge blocks of foam. It is a model for the floating communities the city hopes might one day repopulate the docklands, whose traditional shipping activities are moving elsewhere. Pieter Figdor, one of the pavilion's architects, says floating buildings can be up to seven storeys tall, are inherently floodproof and can easily be moved.

As societies develop they can afford the human and physical infrastructure needed to protect against, and respond to, natural disaster.

Wealth Protection

Making cities more resilient involves starker trade-offs in the developing world. On the one hand, urbanisation strips cities of their natural defences against disaster and exposes more people to loss of life and property when an earthquake or cyclone hits. On the other hand, urbanisation makes poor people richer. The density and infrastructure of cities makes people more productive and more able to afford the measures needed to keep them safe. So mitigation measures should not discourage people from crowding into vulnerable cities but rather establish incentives for cities and their inhabitants to protect themselves better.

Many cities have tough building codes but fail to enforce them. The World Bank study argues that giving more urban dwellers title to their property would encourage investment in their safety, and lifting rent controls would encourage landlords to comply with building codes, since they could then recoup the cost. Ordinary infrastructure can be designed to double as disaster protection, ensuring that it will be properly maintained when the time comes. Two examples the World Bank gives are schools built on higher ground that double as cyclone shelters and a road tunnel in Kuala Lumpur that doubles as a flood-containment tank.

As societies develop they can afford the human and physical infrastructure needed to protect against, and respond to, natural disaster. In time, last year's earthquake and tsunami and floods will be mere blips in the GDP of Japan and Thailand, thanks to the rapid reconstruction made possible by the same wealth that meant the disasters were so costly to start with. The lesson for poorer countries is that growth is the best disaster-mitigation policy of all.

Early Warning Is Insufficient Preparation for Famines in Africa

Jeeyon Janet Kim and Debarati Guha-Sapir

In the following viewpoint, Jeeyon Janet Kim and Debarati Guha-Sapir argue that early warning systems are insufficient to prevent famine in Africa. They report that although alerts of impending food shortages were transmitted in 2010, the international community did not pay attention. By the time the United Nations declared a famine in July 2011, some eleven million people were starving. The authors assert that "early warnings must trigger early response" to effectively prevent the disaster of famine. Kim and Guha-Sapir are researchers at the Centre for Research on the Epidemiology of Disasters at the School of Public Health at the Université catholique de Louvain (UCL) in Belgium.

As you read, consider the following questions:

1. What is the ultimate goal of the early warning systems (EWS), as the authors identify?

2. How many people were expected to be food insecure in 2012 in South Sudan, according to the viewpoint?

Jeeyon Janet Kim and Debarati Guha-Sapir, "Famines in Africa: Is Early Warning Early Enough?," *Global Health Action*, vol. 5, 2012, pp. 1–3. Copyright © 2012 by Co-Action Publishing. All rights reserved. Reproduced by permission.

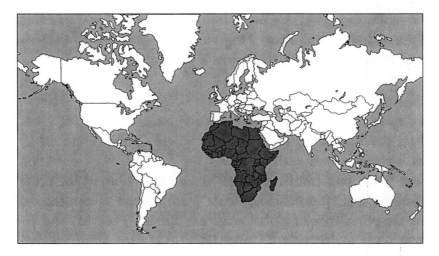

3. According to the viewpoint, what has been shown to save lives and money?

On July 21st, 2011, the *New York Times* headlined 'Food crisis in Somalia is a famine, U.N. [United Nations] says'. It was the first famine declared since 1991–1992 and first significant food crisis in three years. By the time the major global press began to document the food crisis in the Horn of Africa (HOA), however, it was already much too late. Malnutrition and hunger were already widespread in the region affecting over 10 million people and communities had started migrating in search of food.

In 1984–1985, severe famines in Sudan and Ethiopia prompted the international community to put in place early warning systems (EWS) to anticipate and avert future food crises. The Famine Early Warning Systems Network (FEWS NET), for example, has been in place since the mid-eighties to ensure that timely and rigorous early warning and vulnerability information are available. USAID [United States Agency for International Development] budgeted $23 million in 2011 for FEWS NET so that policy makers could readily identify potential threats to food security. Large investments have also been made in other EWS such as the Food and Agriculture

Organization (FAO)'s Global Information and Early Warning System and World Food Programme's Vulnerability Analysis and Mapping Unit, to name just a few.

The ultimate goal of these EWS is to provide decision makers with up-to-date information necessary to avert or mitigate the impact of a food security hazard. FEWS NET utilizes the Integrated Food Security Phase Classification (IPC) as a standardized scale to assess the food security, nutrition and livelihood information to classify the severity of acute food insecurity outcomes. Acute malnutrition is categorized by the prevalence of global acute malnutrition (GAM) and severe acute malnutrition. Under IPC, GAM prevalence between 15–30% is considered a Phase 4 of an 'emergency' while prevalence exceeding 30% is a Phase 5 of a 'catastrophe' or a 'famine'. At Phase 4 levels, the international humanitarian system is triggered into full response mode.

By the time the major global press began to document the food crisis in the Horn of Africa, . . . it was already much too late. Malnutrition and hunger were already widespread.

Overall, several of the functioning EWS performed their task effectively during the recent HOA crisis. As far back as March 2010, surveys began documenting critical rates of acute malnutrition and assessing the overall nutrition status as being critical or very critical across all urban centers scattered throughout the country. By August 2010, there was concern about severe food insecurity developing in east Africa and an impending crisis was forecast. In March 2011, additional warnings were issued on the alarming situation which was expected to deteriorate further. By mid-2011 when famine was finally declared, surveys conducted in the crisis-affected regions of southern Somalia showed that 13 of 18 locations had GAM levels exceeding 30% and all 18 locations had crude mortality rates that exceeded the emergency threshold of 1/10,000 a day. These figures not only surpassed the IPC Phase 4 levels, they also exceeded the IPC Phase 5 or catastrophe or famine level. By this time, FAO estimated that 11 million people were in desperate and immediate need for food.

Aid Was Too Little and Too Late

Despite the wide availability of up-to-date information on the deteriorating conditions in late 2010, humanitarian aid was both sporadic and inadequate. The small increase in aid in early 2011 did little to avert the crisis that unfolded shortly after. There was a surge in aid only when the UN declared famine and media increased their level of coverage of the HOA crisis.

The fact that the response to the East African famine was delayed and inadequate did not go unnoticed.

In light of the suffering afflicted by the drought and delay in response, organizations around the world drafted the Charter to End Extreme Hunger, to seek government commitment to take the steps to prevent suffering of this scale from reoccurring. The Ministers of International Development of Norway, United Kingdom, and the European Commission all declared their support for the charter. The nongovernmental sector also decried the delayed response and called for change.

Despite the wide availability of up-to-date information on the deteriorating conditions in late 2010, humanitarian aid was both sporadic and inadequate.

Unfortunately, the HOA is not the only region today where early warnings did not trigger an early response. In South Sudan, 4.7 million people are expected to be food insecure during 2012 and conditions are deteriorating daily. An estimated 10 million people are also facing food insecurity and over 1 million children are at risk of severe acute malnutrition in the Sahel countries. Facing a serious food and nutrition crisis, Burkina Faso, Chad, Mali, Mauritania and Niger have declared a crisis and called for international assistance. Exacerbated by the conflict-induced displacement in Mali, conditions in the region are worsening and immediate emergency assistance is required to prevent further increases in the rates of malnutrition.

Admittedly, it is difficult to justify and mobilize the humanitarian resources when a situation has not reached critical levels. Yet, if alarms are only sounded when children and other vulnerable populations are already suffering from acute malnutrition and mortality is increasing, the response—however rapid—will be too late.

With the deteriorating food crises in the whole Sahel region and South Sudan, there is an urgent need to institutionalize change now.

Necessary Changes

First, the mechanisms that guide the release of humanitarian funds must be reviewed and modified. Currently, appeals are based on what is programmatically achievable given constraints of access and partners, rather than what is required to avert disasters. The delay in response was further compounded by the UN humanitarian appeal timeline which did not align with the seasons in the HOA. In September 2010 assessments were carried out before October, when the rainy season usually begins. In turn, the assessment failed to take into account the failure of rains and also ignored the predictions of future weather patterns. A further weakness in early assessments is the potential and bias in responders conducting their own evaluations. Given the delay mobilizing funds and getting functional operation on the ground, the Central Emergency [Response] Fund (CERF) [formerly the Central Emergency Revolving Fund] is a useful tool to jump-start response in acute emergencies. Greater reliance on independent and rigor-

Drought in Eastern Africa, 2011

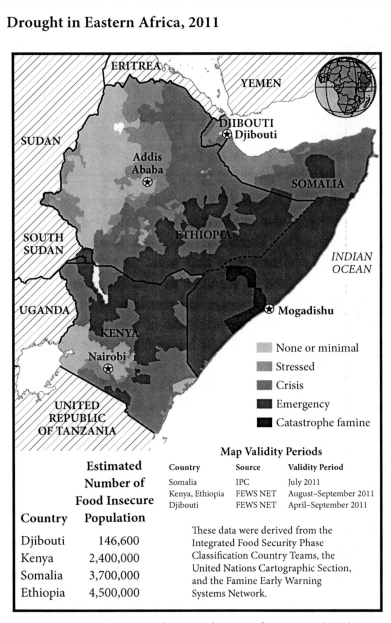

	None or minimal
	Stressed
	Crisis
	Emergency
	Catastrophe famine

Map Validity Periods

Country	Source	Validity Period
Somalia	IPC	July 2011
Kenya, Ethiopia	FEWS NET	August–September 2011
Djibouti	FEWS NET	April–September 2011

These data were derived from the Integrated Food Security Phase Classification Country Teams, the United Nations Cartographic Section, and the Famine Early Warning Systems Network.

Country	Estimated Number of Food Insecure Population
Djibouti	146,600
Kenya	2,400,000
Somalia	3,700,000
Ethiopia	4,500,000

TAKEN FROM: International Livestock Research Institute (ILRI), July 29, 2011.

ous needs assessment could significantly strengthen the appropriate use of funds from CERF. It also needs to be better linked to early warning systems.

If alarms are only sounded when children and other vulnerable populations are already suffering from acute malnutrition and mortality is increasing, the response—however rapid—will be too late.

Second, there is a need to operationalize trigger mechanisms. Certainly, the establishment of standardized triggers and corresponding thresholds may not always work; it is, however, an important step that must be taken to press for early response. Given its mandate to coordinate humanitarian actors in emergency responses and recent support of the charter, the Office for the Coordination of Humanitarian Affairs (OCHA) is well placed to take leadership in these two initiatives. Member states should put in place the required conditions to allow such coordination. The capacity of OCHA to coordinate has been often questioned but not the pertinent need for a multi-lateral coordinating body. In-depth reform of OCHA to strength its credibility, independence and performance is clearly needed and this key humanitarian function should be given priority.

Early Warnings Must Trigger Early Response

In conclusion, timely and effective prevention has been shown to save lives and money. By waiting for a situation to develop into a crisis, like the one in the HOA, children develop severe malnutrition that permanently affects their lives and the stage is set for disease outbreaks, hikes in mortality rates, social tensions, migration and conflicts. Beyond these concerns, there is, most importantly, a moral and ethical imperative for the humanitarian community to act. We must not *wait* for a situation to become a catastrophe; early warnings must trigger early response.

Without Effective Prevention, Natural Hazards Become Human-Made Disasters

The World Bank

In the following viewpoint, writers from the World Bank argue that while earthquakes, droughts, volcanoes, and floods are natural hazards, these hazards become "unnatural disasters" when humans fail to adequately prepare or act in ways that are detrimental to the safety of humankind. They further assert that prevention is a cost-effective way to limit the economic impact of a disaster. For this to take place, however, governments and both public and private interests must accept policy changes and work together to mitigate risk. Governments, in particular, must accept responsibility for the infrastructure of a country. The World Bank is an international economic organization.

As you read, consider the following questions:

1. For what reasons will exposure to hazards rise in cities, according to the viewpoint?

2. What open source software should make the collection and sharing of data easier, in the World Bank's view?

3. When do donors usually respond to disasters?

World Bank, United Nations. 2010. *Natural Hazards, UnNatural Disasters: The Economics of Effective Prevention.* Copyright © The International Bank for Reconstruction and Development/The World Bank. www.gfdrr.org/sites/gfdrr.org/files/nhud/files/NHUD-Overview.pdf. Creative Commons Attribution CC BY 3.0.

The adjective "UnNatural" in [relation to] this report conveys its key message: Earthquakes, droughts, floods, and storms are *natural hazards*, but the *unnatural disasters* are deaths and damages that result from human acts of omission and commission. Every disaster is unique, but each exposes actions—by individuals and governments at different levels—that, had they been different, would have resulted in fewer deaths and less damage. Prevention is possible, and this report examines what it takes to do this cost-effectively.

The report looks at disasters primarily through an economic lens. Economists emphasize self-interest to explain how people choose the amount of prevention, insurance, and coping. But lenses can distort as well as sharpen images, so the report also draws from other disciplines: psychology to examine how people may misperceive risks, political science to understand voting patterns, and nutrition science to see how stunting in children after a disaster impairs cognitive abilities and productivity as adults much later. Peering into the future, the report shows that growing cities will increase exposure to hazards, but that vulnerability will not rise if cities are better managed. The intensities and frequencies of hazards in the coming decades will change with the climate, and the report examines this complicated and contentious subject, acknowledging all the limitations of data and science.

Four Main Findings

First, a disaster exposes the cumulative implications of many earlier decisions, some taken individually, others collectively, and a few by default. A deeper questioning of what happened, and why, could prevent a repetition of disasters. Several factors usually contribute to any disaster, some less obvious than others. The immediate cause of a bridge or building collapse may be a mudslide, though poor design or construction may have also contributed. But the underlying cause may be denuded hillsides that increased sediment flows (as in Haiti), or poor urban planning that put the bridge or building in harm's way. Symptoms are easily mistaken for cause: Denuded hillsides may result from desperately poor people depleting the vegetation to survive or from logging concessions that encourage tree cutting but not planting. Effective prevention measures are therefore not always "obvious."

Second, prevention is often possible and cost-effective. Studies for the report examined the costs and benefits of specific prevention measures that homeowners could take in hazard-prone areas of four low- and middle-income countries. Prevention pays for assumed (but reasonable) costs and discount rates. Other prevention measures are embedded in infrastructure (such as adequate drainage ditches). The report examines government expenditures on prevention and finds that it is generally lower than relief spending, which rises after a disaster and remains high for several subsequent years. But effective prevention depends not just on the amount but on what funds are spent on. For example, Bangladesh reduced deaths from cyclones by spending modest sums on shelters, developing accurate weather forecasts, issuing warnings that people heeded, and arranging for their evacuation. All this cost less than building large-scale embankments that would have been less effective.

Every disaster is unique, but each exposes actions—by individuals and governments at different levels—that, had they been different, would have resulted in fewer deaths and less damage.

Third, many measures—private and public—must work well together for effective prevention. Low-lying areas around Jakarta illustrate the complexity of ensuring this: Residents raise the plinth of their houses to protect against floods, but they also draw water through bore wells causing the ground to subside. Even knowing this, a person has no choice if the government does not provide piped water. So, the prevention measures an individual undertakes also depend on what the government does—or fails to do—and vice versa.

That many measures do not work well together in poor countries explains why they have more disasters. The poor may know the hazard risks they face but depend more on public services that are often inadequate. They live near work on cheaper land exposed to hazards if buses are unreliable, while the rich with cars have better alternatives. The poor would willingly move to safer locations if their incomes rose or if public transport became more reliable. Many governments in poor countries struggle to provide such services, and until they do, the poor will remain vulnerable.

Fourth, the exposure to hazards will rise in cities, but greater exposure need not increase vulnerability. Large cities exposed to cyclones and earthquakes will more than double their population by 2050 (from 680 million in 2000 to 1.5 billion in 2050). The increase will differ by country and region. Vulnerability need not increase with exposure if cities are well managed, but the projected increase in exposure underscores the enormous task ahead.

Urban growth is not the only concern. Climate change has received much attention, and there are urgent calls for immediate action because the effects of climate change are cumulative and felt much later. The "World Development Report 2010" discusses the implications of climate change in detail; this report is limited to its *direct* effects on hazards. One estimate of the increase in damage associated with changed tropical cyclone activity as a result of climate change is between $28 billion and $68 billion annually by 2100. This represents an increase of between 50 and 125 percent over no climate change. There is considerable uncertainty around these long-term projections, reflecting the limits of the data and the climate models that generate them. The damage is in "expected value" terms, but averages hide extremes: A very rare and powerful cyclone could strike a highly vulnerable location causing extremely high damages. And the effects are likely to be concentrated: Several small island countries in the Caribbean are particularly vulnerable.

These four findings are not actionable prescriptions. Many people must do numerous things better, but getting them to do so is the challenge. A successful policy response for effective prevention includes information, interventions, and infrastructure. Underpinning this policy response is the role of "institutions," without which any policy response would be ineffectual. Governments can do much to promote prevention—in line with the policy implications outlined next.

Policy Implications for Governments and Donors

First, governments can and should make information more easily accessible. People are often guided in their prevention decisions by information on hazards, yet the seemingly simple act of collecting and providing information is sometimes a struggle. While some countries attempt to collect and archive their hazard data, efforts are generally inconsistent or insufficient. Specifically, there are no universal standards for archiving environmental parameters for defining hazards and related data. Data exchange, hazard analysis, and hazard mapping thus become difficult. . . . Few countries collect and archive data on hazards—even though technological advances such as the abundance of free, simple, and open source software (for example, PostGIS, GeoServer, MapServer, the GeoNode.org project) should make collecting and sharing information easy.

And where information is collected, it is not always shared, even though sharing information on hazards involves relatively little expense because some government agencies already collect and analyze data on hazard risks. Those preparing background papers for this report had difficulties obtaining disaster and related data from various public agencies and universities, even though donors often funded the collection and automation of disaster data. Sometimes "security, commercial, and defense" reasons are invoked, but only a few are legitimate. Sometimes commercial interests take precedence over public good aspects.

A successful policy response for effective prevention includes information, interventions, and infrastructure.

So, the importance of making information about hazard risks available cannot be overemphasized. Perhaps because of this significance, the political will to not have information on rising levels of risk publicized is often strong. For example, even though the Federal Emergency Management Agency (FEMA) in the United States has updated coastal flood maps for the U.S. Gulf, it cannot get coastal communities to accept them because the information would reduce property prices. Systematic mechanisms for tracking information related to the changing nature of risk, and translating it into risk-related property valuations, would go a long way to increase the incentives for prevention. Making maps of floodplains and seismic fault lines easily accessible would make developers and property owners more aware of the risks—and more motivated to build appropriately. Collecting data on weather and climate is also integral to producing accurate forecasts.

Second, governments should permit land and housing markets to work, supplementing them with targeted interventions when necessary. When land and housing markets work, property values reflect hazard risks, guiding people's decisions on where to live and what prevention measures to take. Detailed empirical work for this report matched some 800,000 buildings in Bogota that differed in their exposure to seismic risk to a range of characteristics (such as size, construction quality, distance from the city center, and whether residential, commercial, or industrial). Because the only difference among comparable properties is their level of hazard risk, this allowed assessing whether property values are lower in riskier areas. . . .

But markets, when smothered, dampen the incentives for prevention. In Mumbai, where rent controls have been pervasive, property owners have neglected maintenance for decades, so buildings crumble in heavy rains. Rent controls are not unique to Mumbai or developing countries. Rent control laws have remained in place in some form in New York City since 1943, where there are currently about a million rent-regulated and 50,000 rent-controlled apartments. As recently as 2009, legislation was passed in New York that limits the ability of landlords statewide to increase rents. Such laws are expected to return to regulation many household units previously attracting market rents. They exist in about 40 countries, including many developed countries. And rent controls are not the only market distortion. Real estate transactions in many countries incur a tax on sales, not on owning property. But taxing transactions reduces property sales and encourages undervaluation. And restrictions on cement prices and imports can create black markets and exorbitant prices, so that adulterated cement ends up weakening structures.

Getting land and rental markets to work can go a long way to inducing people to locate in appropriate areas and take preventive measures. But this will not be a straightforward task. Nor will it be easy to remove the panoply of market distortions because many benefit vested interests. And knowing what to change first is not obvious. Past policies weigh heavily on the present: Many structures now standing were built earlier, and defects are difficult to detect and harder to remedy. A corollary is that correcting policies now will not result in immediate improvements, though correcting them sooner would be better than delaying. Where new construction dominates, as in developing countries' urban areas, this legacy is less of an issue, but wealthier countries also bear this burden: Mispriced insurance (premia too low because of populist pressures on a regulated industry) has led to overbuilding along the hurricane-prone U.S. coastline.

The poor bear the brunt of the cumulative effects of such policies (tax structure, city financing arrangements, and so on) which produce only a limited and unresponsive supply of affordable, legal land sites for safer housing. Governments could greatly expand the choices of the poor—who often locate in dangerous areas and slums exposed to hazards—but this is more subtle than dictating what they should choose. Poor households prefer to have easier access to jobs, even though this may imply living in slums on riverbanks prone to flooding or on hilltops subject to mudslides. In some cases, security of property (clear titles often help) allows people to invest in prevention measures. When the social consequences of settling in hazardous zones are so adverse, the correct response is for governments to make targeted interventions. This could include making land available in safer locations—along with adequate and reliable public transport and other services so that people remain connected to their jobs.

Governments Must Provide Adequate Infrastructure

Third, governments must provide adequate infrastructure and other public services, and multipurpose infrastructure holds promise. Much prevention is embedded in infrastructure, but effectiveness depends on quality. Infrastructure needs maintenance: fixing potholes in the road before the winter or the rains; painting steel bridges before they weaken through corrosion; inspecting and fixing cracks in concrete bridges. All engineers know this, but they do not always obtain budget appropriations—even in the United States, where the 2007 bridge collapse in Minneapolis drew attention to such neglect.

Spending should go down a list arranged in descending order of (economic) rates of return. But when subject to arbitrary budget spending limits and lumpiness, low-return spending often gets put ahead of postponable high-return spending. Since maintenance can be postponed, it gets deferred—repeatedly—until the asset crumbles. Drainage ditches, once built, are not adequately maintained and become clogged; so rains result in floods that drown the poor. Other less obvious public services include reliable city transport, and these require better—not always more—public spending. For example, about 30 percent of infrastructure assets of a typical African country need rehabilitation, and just $0.6 billion on road maintenance would yield $2.6 billion in annual benefits.

Much prevention is embedded in infrastructure, . . . [which] needs maintenance: fixing potholes in the road before the winter or the rains; painting steel bridges before they weaken . . . ; inspecting and fixing cracks in concrete bridges.

Governments must ensure that new infrastructure does not introduce new risk. This is particularly important since, in many developing countries, infrastructure investment—long-lived capital stock—is likely to peak in the coming few decades. Locating infrastructure out of harm's way is one way of doing so. Where that may not be possible, another way is to execute multipurpose infrastructure projects, such as Kuala Lumpur's Stormwater Management and Road Tunnel (SMART). Floods from heavy rains are a hazard, and the 9.7 kilometers long $514 million tunnel has three levels, the lowest for drainage and the upper two for road traffic. The drain allows large volumes of floodwater to be diverted from the city's financial district to a storage reservoir, holding pond, and bypass tunnel. Combining the drain with the road has two advantages: It ensures maintenance of a drain that otherwise would be used only sporadically, and it costs less than building each separately.

Infrastucture, even when well designed, constructed, and maintained, cannot always prevent disasters. Governments must, therefore, pay heed to a subset of "critical infrastructure" that once selected, is subject to higher than usual "margins of safety" (the extra strength that engineers build into designs). Such critical infrastructure must be identified before a disaster to ensure its adequacy. But what is critical is situation specific—safe schools serve as cyclone shelters in Bangladesh, but hospitals (not schools) may be more critical in Turkey to treat crushed limbs when buildings collapse in earthquakes. And governments must be careful about keeping the list short: When it includes too many assets, the costs rise without commensurate benefits. Even the United States encounters difficulties in keeping critical infrastructure manageably small, and other governments will undoubtedly discover this as well.

The Importance of Public Oversight

Fourth, good institutions must develop to permit public oversight. Good institutions both reflect and create prosperity, and one robust finding of this report is that countries with well-performing institutions are better able to prevent disasters, including reducing the likelihood of disaster-related conflict. But institutions transcend specific entities. Parliaments, media, business associations, and the like function differently across countries—even if they have similar legal authority and responsibilities.

Fostering good institutions means letting evolve a messy array of overlapping entities (the media, neighborhood associations, engineering groups) that may not all have lofty motives but nevertheless allow divergent views to percolate into the public consciousness. Permitting dissent allows the public to be informed and involved when alternative proposals and opposing views compete for their support. Public involvement and oversight ensure that good ideas are considered even if they are unusual (Kuala Lumpur's dual-use drain and car tunnel). Such oversight also encourages communities to experiment with, and to devise, their own sustainable arrangements that promote prevention.

Where institutions have been suppressed, results are discouraging. Storm damage is more severe in Haiti than in the adjoining Dominican Republic. Deforestation is the visible difference but the quality of institutions is the less visible one. Haiti's institutions and communities have withered from decades of misrule. Vibrant communities help ensure that trees are not thoughtlessly felled and that saplings planted will grow. Even if the interest of uplanders who cut the trees may diverge from lowlanders who get the mud flows, communities bridge these differences and manage the fair use of the commons. Prosperity ultimately depends on rebuilding the trust and social capital that was lost even before the earthquakes and hurricanes struck.

Public involvement and oversight ensure that good ideas are considered even if they are unusual.

Good Institutions Increase Safety

Often, institutions are linked to democracy, but this report finds that it is not the label of democracy or dictatorship that matters. Good institutions are associated with political competition more than voting alone (the conventional understanding of democracy). Across both nondemocracies and democracies, the existence of "institutionalized" political parties—parties that allow members to discipline leaders who pursue policies at odds with member interests—is significantly associated with reductions in disaster mortality. The mortality from earthquakes falls by 6 percent for an additional year of competitive elections, and by 2 percent when the average party age rises by a year. Such systems are therefore more likely to respond to citizens' needs.

Preventing disasters requires many public and private agencies to work well together, and governments could play an institutional role in this. But there is no single recipe for strengthening institutions; a wide variety of political systems can serve the purpose. But encouraging a diverse set of organizations that facilitate collective action by large groups of citizens will allow them to press more effectively for the spread of information, the availability of prevention measures and alternatives, and their cost-effectiveness.

The Importance of Donors

And fifth, donors have a role in prevention as well. The report's overarching theme is that not enough is being done on prevention. Donors usually respond to disasters after they strike: About a fifth of total humanitarian aid between 2000 and 2008 was devoted to spending on disaster relief and response.

The share of humanitarian funding going to prevention is small but increasing—from about 0.1 percent in 2001 to 0.7 percent in 2008. However, prevention activities often imply long-term development expenditures whereas the focus of humanitarian aid—already a tiny part of official development aid—is immediate relief and response. Donors concerned with prevention could earmark official development aid (rather than humanitarian aid) for prevention-related activities. And such aid, if used effectively, could reduce issues arising from the Samaritan's dilemma: the inability to deny help following a disaster to those who have not taken sufficient prevention measures.

Lack of Preparation for Floods in Brazil Leads to Many Deaths

Natalia Viana

In the following viewpoint, Natalia Viana reports on terrible floods that occurred in January 2011 in Brazil. Over eight hundred people died, and many were left homeless. Viana argues that Brazil's growing cities are unprepared for heavy rains and the resulting floods and mudslides that are becoming worse each year. The lack of preparation is because the government is preoccupied with winning elections, the author asserts, rather than long-term planning. The lack of preparation makes large numbers of people vulnerable for death or injury. Viana is an independent Brazilian journalist.

As you read, consider the following questions:

1. How many people died in the state of São Paolo during heavy rains?
2. How will most of the money released for disaster containment be spent, as Viana reports?
3. What are "piscinões"?

Natalia Viana, "Floods in Brazil Are a Result of Short-Term Planning," *The Guardian Poverty Blog*, February 2, 2011. Reproduced by permission.

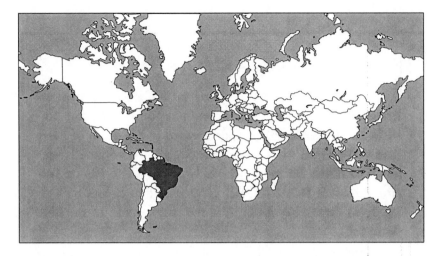

As I write [February 2, 2011], more than two weeks after the floods began in the mountainous region of Rio de Janeiro state, many communities remain isolated due to landslides on the main access roads.

More than 800 people died and thousands of people have been displaced in the state, according to official figures. One of the worst affected towns is Santa Rita. Dozens of families still depend on helicopters to deliver food, water, and emergency health care. In the town of Teresópolis, people are starting to clear debris in the streets by hand, with shovels and brushes. And in Nova Friburgo, families watch, and cry, as their homes are demolished.

In the neighbouring state of São Paulo, the richest in the country, 25 people died because of the heavy rains. In Santa Catarina state, in the south, five people lost their lives and 17,000 had to flee their homes.

The January rains in Brazil are becoming more severe and floods are becoming a routine. But while specialists say it's too early to confirm the heavy rains are caused by climate change, the fact is that Brazilian cities have never been ready for them.

Brazil Is at High Risk for Floods

A series of floods and mudslides in January 2011 demonstrated the high degree of flash and river flood risks that Brazil faces. The January 13 floods resulted in the death of more than 800 people, while about 100,000 people became homeless. The floods hit mostly the hilly towns above Rio de Janeiro. President Dilma Roussef confirmed that homes built illegally in these risky areas were the major cause of the high death toll.

Floods and landslides are not rare events in the country; they are frequent and widespread across Brazil. In the past decade, 37 disastrous floods happened while about 5 million people were affected by the rain-related disasters over the last two decades. On average, 120 people die a year as a result of major floods in the past decade. The floods also generated high levels of economic loss. For instance, the 2004 floods in 15 states caused 300 million dollars in losses; the 2008 flooding in Santa Catarina did 400 million dollars in damages, and the April 2009 floods caused losses of 500 million. About 10 percent of the population (19 million) is exposed to river flood risks, while 14 percent are at risk to flash floods.

Engin Ibrahim Erdem,
"Flood Risk and Tenure Regularization in Brazil,"
Florida International University, 2011. http://digitalcommons.fiu.edu
/cgi/viewcontent.cgi?article=1005&context=drr_student.

Brazil's Cities Are Unprepared

Urban planning has never been part of the political agenda.

Governments react, rather than plan and prevent. The ministry in charge of monitoring urban planning, the Ministry of Cities, was only created in 2003. The Supreme Court is still deciding if all cities will have to set out and follow an urban plan as defined in 1988 in [the] new federal constitution.

But nothing has changed. Just after the floods, the government said it would set up a national system to prevent disasters—which won't be fully working for four years.

The Plano de Aceleração do Crescimento (PAC)—the national "plan of growth acceleration"—released two years ago as the major project for infrastructure works, provides about £4.4bn [about $7 billion] for disaster containment. Most will be used for drainage, but containment caps for hills will also be built.

"These are emergency works purely to reduce the repetition of tragedies," says Celso Carvalho, the national secretary of urban programmes. "Our cities are very insecure because of the failure to apply urban planning."

The reason urban planning was never taken into account is simple: The expression "long-term planning" is rarely found in Brazil's political dictionary. Short-term, eye-catching public works are the focus. Winning elections is the aim. Dominated by this logic, the main driver of cities' growth is profit, above everything else.

That's the reason why so many people live in high-risk areas, such as the slopes of mountains. Land in the city centres is too valuable for social housing; often governments don't force the private sector to use land in this way.

"The Brazilian cities' comprehensive plan puts forward measures to avoid this problem, such as the creation of social interest zones and progressive taxing of unoccupied or sub-utilised buildings. The problem is that the pressure from estate agents is too high. Governments tend to yield to that," says Nabil Bonduki, a professor at the University of São Paulo and former city councillor. Building contractors and real estate companies are among some of the biggest campaign donors as well.

The Problem Is Extensive

"The real challenge is just how deep-rooted and extensive the problem is. A [principle of] laissez-faire rules [with little authoritative intervention] in our cities, producing not only risky territories occupied by poor people, but also some risk areas occupied by the upper classes," says Luiz Cesar de Queiroz Ribeiro, a professor at the Federal University of Rio de Janeiro and coordinator of the Observatory of Metropolitan Cities. In Rio, many of the houses that came down in the landslides belonged to middle-class families. They lived in risky areas because the views were good, the location was beautiful and the public administrators didn't have the strength to move them out. For Ribeiro, the institutional fragility of local administrations led to an incomplete process of citizenship building—for rich and poor.

The reason urban planning was never taken into account is simple: The expression "long-term planning" is rarely found in Brazil's political dictionary. Short-term, eye-catching public works are the focus.

The city of São Paulo is a good example. Every summer, thousands of people are affected by flooding, mainly in the poor neighbourhoods. About 10,000 people live in areas that are most affected—and the number is growing. Large avenues can become canals as widespread paving and impermeable soil leave little space for water drainage. The main government measure is to build "piscinões"—large reservoirs to retain water and stop it from running into rivers, so reducing the flow. And add to that the new roadway that was quickly built in the avenue that borders the Tietê River, one of the busiest roads in the city, to absorb traffic—paving the small bits of land that were left to absorb rainwater.

"Public works can't be done in 24 hours," says Geraldo Alckmin, the governor of São Paulo, now starting his second term in office.

So that's the logic behind it. Urban planners rarely think beyond the four-year term of an elected administration. Then, when a new governor takes office, his or her first measure is to discontinue all major policies in place. New administrators will sometimes rename all projects in an effort to claim credit for them.

It is a common saying that Brazilians don't have good memories. Our governments work hard to ensure it.

Japan Was Unprepared for the 2011 Earthquake and Tsunami

Jun Hongo

In the following viewpoint, Jun Hongo reports that many earthquake experts believed Japan was unprepared for a large earthquake and tsunami, although historically the country has had many such events, including an 1896 tsunami that took more than twenty-two thousand lives. The damage caused by the 2011 earthquake and tsunami was extensive, Hongo asserts, and the greatest disaster in Japan since World War II. Nevertheless, experts believe Japan could have mitigated the damage by paying attention to history and better preparing for a large amount of water. Hongo is a reporter for the Japan Times.

As you read, consider the following questions:

1. In what three years was Japan visited by killer tsunami waves, according to the viewpoint?
2. What happened when news of Tokyo tap water being contaminated with iodine-131 reached residents, as Hongo reports?
3. What is one key reconstruction goal for the Tohoku region, according to the viewpoint?

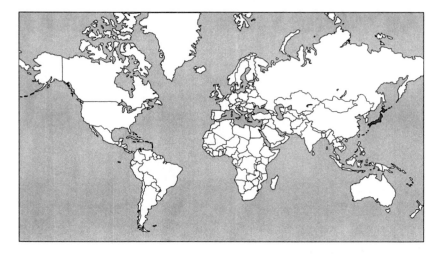

A month after [in April 2011] the earthquake and tsunami obliterated cities along the Tohoku coast, Japan is struggling to limp back to some semblance of normalcy while coming to grips with the unprecedented disaster.

But critics say the country could have done more to mitigate the catastrophe.

"The tsunami and the earthquake were bigger than anything I have experienced," said Ryohei Morimoto, an honorary member of the Association for Earthquake Disaster Prevention and a retired professor of volcanology at the University of Tokyo.

But he also pointed out that March 11 wasn't the first time the northeast Pacific coast was visited by killer waves, including tsunami in 1611, 1896 and 1933. The geographical characteristics of the bays can amplify tsunami, such as the waves that hit in 1896, taking more than 22,000 lives.

The Government Should Have Prepared

"I've heard the government and Tokyo Electric Power Co. say they couldn't predict the tsunami would reach that high, but that is ridiculous," Morimoto said, noting any history book would have set them straight.

"And even if they couldn't predict the size of tsunami, they should have at least prepared for waves similar to those in the past," Morimoto said.

Critics say [Japan] could have done more to mitigate the catastrophe.

According to the National Police Agency [NPA], the tsunami and the magnitude 9.0 earthquake—the fifth-largest earthquake to occur on the planet since 1900—had so far left 13,116 confirmed dead as of Monday and 14,377 missing—the first disaster since the war to claim more than 10,000 casualties in Japan.

The NPA also said 48,747 homes were destroyed, 56 bridges damaged and four breakwaters collapsed due to the events on March 11 [2011]. Over 150,000 people are living in evacuation shelters throughout northeastern Japan, they added.

The extent of the damage prompted Emperor Akihito to record his first public message since the late Emperor Hirohito addressed the nation on Aug. 15, 1945, to announce Japan's surrender.

"I would like to let you know how deeply touched I am by the courage of those victims who have survived this catastrophe and who, by bracing themselves, are demonstrating their determination to live on," the Emperor said March 16 in the unprecedented TV address.

A Record Earthquake

The Tohoku earthquake was one for the record books.

According to the Earthquake Research Institute at the University of Tokyo, [the] March 11 tsunami reached as high as 37.9 meters [124 feet] in Taro, Iwate Prefecture. The tallest ever to hit was the 38.2-meter [125 feet] wave that destroyed the Iwate city of Ofunato following an 8.5-magnitude temblor in 1896.

The Japan Coast Guard also revealed last week that the seabed at the epicenter of the quake, located approximately 13 km [8 miles] off Miyagi Prefecture, slid 24 meters [42 feet] and rose up 3 meters [almost 10 feet], based on its study. In total, the quake shifted Honshu more than 2 meters [6.5 feet] eastward, according to their research.

To top off the seismic impact, a survey by NASA's [National Aeronautics and Space Administration's] Jet Propulsion Laboratory revealed that the intense shift of the earth's crust changed the distribution of the planet's mass. Because of the way the fault responsible for the quake slipped, the earth now rotates faster, making a day about 1.8 microseconds shorter than before.

How a country gets back on its feet after such a cataclysm remains to be seen, even though Japan, which lays atop different layers of tectonic plates, has survived similar disasters.

The 7.9-magnitude Great Hanshin Earthquake in January 1995 resulted in the loss of 6,434 lives, destroyed more than 100,000 houses and caused an estimated ¥10 trillion [about 127 billion USD] in damage. The port of Kobe wasn't able to declare it had recovered from the disaster until May 1997.

Picking Up the Pieces

Some Tohoku areas have been quick to pick up the pieces.

East Nippon Expressway Co. said March 22 it had finished emergency repairs to the region's highways that merely days before were impassable. Japan Railways is also scheduled to complete restoration and begin running trains between Tokyo and Sendai within the week.

On the other hand, restoration of basic infrastructure has only just begun. In the city of Ishinomaki in Miyagi Prefecture, where roughly 18,000 people were living in evacuation shelters, only 137 temporary homes were under construction as of April 1, and 3,145 households had already applied for the units, the city said.

How a country gets back on its feet after such a cataclysm remains to be seen.

One factor that differentiates the Hanshin and Tohoku disasters is the timing of the temblor.

The Hanshin quake struck just before 6 A.M., when most people were at home and in bed.

The March 11 earthquake struck at 2:46 P.M. Children were in school, parents were at work and families were separated. Miyagi Prefecture said April 1 that 16 people under age 18 were listed as having lost both parents. The number in Iwate has topped 50 and is expected to grow. The welfare ministry said last week it has already tallied 82 kids who became orphans in the disaster.

A Large Nuclear Disaster

Then there is the nuclear disaster that has affected not only those living in the region but has the international community in panic mode. Due to the contamination of seawater, fish caught anywhere near Japan, even those far away from Fukushima Prefecture, have been shunned at the market.

Because of the damaged nuclear plants, Tokyo Electric Power Co. on March 14 was left to launch rolling blackouts, causing a transportation crisis in the capital and halting factory operations within the region. A week later news of Tokyo tap water being contaminated with iodine-131 broke. Bottled water flew off the shelves in supermarkets while embassies and foreigners chose to evacuate from Japan.

Yet, while many lined up at the Tokyo Immigration Bureau to prepare for departure, others gave a helping hand from overseas in times of need.

The Nuclear Risk from the Great East Japan Earthquake

While the earthquake and tsunami were responsible for the large-scale loss of life and damage to infrastructure, it was the threat posed by damage to nuclear reactors that caused the greatest fear—and the greatest criticism of the Japanese government's response. The earthquake and tsunami created the worst global nuclear crisis since the 1986 Chernobyl disaster. The three active reactor units, reactors 1, 2 and 3 at the Fukushima Daiichi Nuclear Power Station suffered meltdowns after the quake knocked out the plant's power and the tsunami disabled the backup generators meant to keep the cooling systems working. (Reactor units 4–6 were shut down for planned maintenance when the disaster happened.)

Elizabeth Ferris and Daniel Petz, The Year That Shook the Rich: A Review of Natural Disasters in 2011, *Brookings Institution–London School of Economics, March 2012.*

The Japanese Red Cross said it had received ¥139 billion [1.75 billion USD] from 1.5 million donations as of April 5. In contrast, it took over a year after the Hanshin quake for donations to surpass ¥100 billion [1.25 billion USD], the group said. UNICEF [United Nations Children's Fund] also began raising funds for children in Japan, something it had not done since 1964.

Over 20 countries and regions, including China, South Korea and Russia, dispatched emergency rescue teams to the Tohoku region.

But support from the United States, including Operation Tomodachi, a U.S. military relief effort, saw the unprecedented engagement of approximately 14,000 service members, many from the 7th Fleet, working to aid the people hit by the quake.

The U.S. Marine Corps Chemical Biological Incident Response Force last week joined the response to the emergency at the Fukushima No. 1 nuclear plant and is standing by at Yokota Air Base.

The list of lessons to be learned from March 11 is long. At the top, however, is being prepared and taking preventive steps against natural disasters, former University of Tokyo professor Morimoto said.

Seismologists agree the Tokai region could soon see a major temblor with a magnitude of around 8.0 that could cause damage similar to the Tohoku quake or the one that hit the Mino region in 1891. That earthquake over a century ago saw a fault line push the ground 6 meters [about 18 feet] higher than it was.

But Prime Minister Naoto Kan's administration appears clueless on what steps to take.

"Liquefaction was a major issue in the city of Urayasu (Chiba Prefecture) following the March 11 earthquake, which proves landfill and man-made ground are extremely vulnerable to earthquakes," Morimoto said.

The list of lessons to be learned from March 11 [2011] is long. At the top, however, is being prepared and taking preventive steps against natural disasters.

Still, Kan on April 1 said one key reconstruction goal for the Tohoku region will be creating coastal areas with high ground for relocating neighborhoods to prevent further damage from the sea.

"It sounds like a bad idea to me," Morimoto said. "I feel that lessons aren't really being learned."

In the United States, Transportation Planners Were Not Prepared for Hurricane Katrina

Todd Litman

In the following viewpoint, Todd Litman asserts that failures in planning and emergency response resulted in far more deaths than necessary during Hurricane Katrina. Further, Litman argues that although the storm was a natural hazard, it became a disaster only because of significant preparation failures. Specifically, people in New Orleans without cars were not provided for. Worse, Litman writes, "The little effort that was made to assist non-drivers was careless and incompetent." He concludes that hundreds of deaths could have been avoided and much property preserved with adequate planning. Litman is the founder and executive director of the Victoria Transport Policy Institute in British Columbia.

As you read, consider the following questions:

1. How does Litman say buses could have been helpful if they had been given priority in traffic during the forty-eight-hour evacuation period?

Todd Litman, "Lessons from Katrina and Rita: What Major Disasters Can Teach Transportation Planners," Victoria Transport Policy Institute, April 13, 2006, pp. 3, 5–6. Copyright © 2006 by Victoria Transport Policy Institute. All rights reserved. Reproduced by permission.

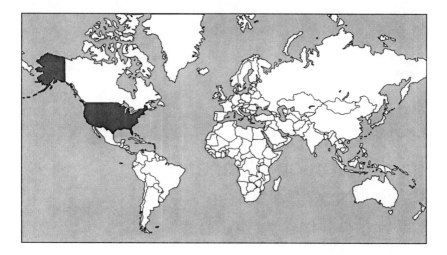

2. How many buses did Mayor Ray Nagin say he needed on September 1, 2005?

3. How is public transit viewed in most North American cities, according to the viewpoint?

It would be wrong to claim that this disaster was an unavoidable "act of god." Katrina began as a hurricane but only became a disaster because of significant, preventable planning and management failures. By most accounts, automobile evacuation functioned adequately. The plan, which involved using all lanes on major highways to accommodate outbound vehicle traffic, was well engineered and publicized. Motorists were able to flee the city, although congestion resulted in very slow traffic speeds and problems when vehicles ran out of fuel or had other mechanical problems.

No Plan for Those Without Cars

However, there was no effective plan to evacuate transit-dependent residents. In an article titled "Planning for the Evacuation of New Orleans" published in the *Institute of Transportation Engineers Journal* the author explains,

Of the 1.4 million inhabitants in the high-threat areas, it is assumed only approximately 60 percent of the population or about 850,000 people will want, or be able, to leave the city. The reasons are numerous. Although the primary reasons are a lack of transportation (it is estimated that about 200,000 to 300,000 people do not have access to reliable personal transportation), an unwillingness to leave homes and property (estimated to be at least 100,000 people) and a lack of outbound roadway capacity.

This indicates that public officials were aware of and willing to accept significant risk to hundreds of thousands of residents unable to evacuate because they lacked transportation. The little effort that was made to assist non-drivers was careless and incompetent. Public officials provided little guidance or assistance to people who lacked automobiles. The city established ten pickup locations where city buses were to take people to emergency shelters, but the service was unreliable. Transit-dependent people were directed to the Superdome, although it had insufficient water, food, medical care and security. This led to a medical and humanitarian crisis. . . .

Public Buses and Trains Were Not Used

The New Orleans Regional Transit Authority (RTA) had a hurricane evacuation policy: Drivers should evacuate buses and other agency vehicles with their families and transit-dependent residents, thereby protecting people and vehicles. There are unconfirmed stories that Amtrak offered use of a train for evacuation that was not accepted by local officials. But neither public buses nor trains were deployed to evacuate people out of the city. Residents who wanted to leave the area by public transport were expected to pay for commercial services, a major barrier to many low-income residents. New Orleans Mayor Ray Nagin later explained that, in his interpretation, using buses to transport residents to the Superdome reflected the emergency plans' intent, and there were insufficient buses to evacuate everybody who needed assistance.

Katrina began as a hurricane but only became a disaster because of significant, preventable planning and management failures.

The city had approximately 500 transit and school buses, a quarter of the estimated 2,000 buses needed to evacuate residents who wanted transport (even more buses would have been needed to carry *all* residents who needed transport, since under emergency conditions it is unrealistic for a bus to carry 50 passengers). However, if given priority in traffic, buses could have made multiple trips out of the city during the 48-hour evacuation period, and even evacuating 10,000 to 30,000 people would have reduced emergency shelter overcrowding. Many public buses were subsequently ruined by the flooding. . . .

The importance of buses for evacuation of the city became clear soon after the hurricane hit. On September 1 Mayor Nagin said on a local radio station, "I need 500 buses. . . This is a national disaster. Get every doggone Greyhound bus line in the country and get their asses moving to New Orleans." Two weeks after the hurricane he explained on NBC's *Meet the Press*:

> Sure, there was [sic] lots of buses out there, but guess what? You can't find drivers that would stay behind with a Category 5 hurricane, you know, pending down on New Orleans. We barely got enough drivers to move people on Sunday, or Saturday and Sunday, to move them to the Superdome. We barely had enough drivers for that. So sure, we had the assets, but the drivers just weren't available.

This indicates that bus deployment was ad hoc, implemented by officials during the emergency without a detailed action plan. Such a plan would include the designation of certain staff as *essential*, meaning that they are expected to work during emergency situations. Transit agency staff would have an incentive to volunteer for such a role because they would be allowed to evacuate their own families.

It is unsurprising that public officials directed transit-dependent residents to local emergency shelters, since that strategy had worked successfully during previous hurricanes. They appeared to be unaware of Katrina's greater severity, and insensitive to the risks and discomfort shelter occupants faced. A more cautious and compassionate plan would have offered all residents the option of free transport out of the city.

The Problems Faced by Non-Drivers

This situation is simply an extreme example of the problems non-drivers face every day. In most North American cities, New Orleans included, public transit is considered a mode of last resort or a novelty for tourists. Service quality is minimal and poorly integrated into the overall transport system. The result is a huge difference in convenience, comfort, and safety between motorists and non-motorists (and therefore between wealthy and poor, white and black, able and disabled), which is degrading and inequitable. It is also inefficient and leads to additional problems, such as costly and dangerous rescue efforts, health problems, and distrust of authority.

With better planning, hundreds of deaths could have been avoided and billions of dollars in property and productivity could have been preserved.

After the hurricane there was no lack of material or human resources ready for deployment. Water, food, state-of-the-art equipment, and skilled rescuers were available and waiting, but were turned back, misdirected or misused. Civil organiza-

The Government's Failure to Prepare for Katrina

Perhaps the most unsettling element to the Hurricane Katrina disaster is the way it happened—not as a silver shadow streaking across the sky but as a massive, lumbering tempest that signaled its intentions days before following through. There were no dramatic fireballs, no sudden flashes of light, no buildings that fell to vapor over the course of an hour or so. Hurricane Katrina traveled toward its destination at roughly walking speed, giving federal officials days to plot a counterstrategy. If intelligence drives Homeland Security's disaster-response planning and execution, few calamities provide better advance intelligence than a hurricane. Storm surges can be modeled, wind speed can be measured, and landfall is a predictable event. Yet, as Katrina moved through the Gulf of Mexico, the department reacted with far less determination than it had during a myriad of false terrorist alarms in the months and years before. Indeed, in 2004 the agency had included a hurricane strike in New Orleans in its pantheon of most-feared disasters, right up there with a nuclear attack and a plot to sabotage the nation's food supply. Yet as Katrina approached, Washington [DC] seemed to go dark in the face of clear catastrophe.

Christopher Cooper and Robert Block, Disaster: Hurricane Katrina and the Failure of Homeland Security. *New York: Henry Holt, 2006, p. xv.*

tions were not allowed into the city to provide assistance. The American Red Cross explained soon after the hurricane struck (2005),

Access to New Orleans is controlled by the National Guard and local authorities and while we are in constant contact with them, we simply cannot enter New Orleans against their orders. The state Homeland Security Department had requested—and continues to request—that the American Red Cross not come back into New Orleans following the hurricane. Our presence would keep people from evacuating and encourage others to come into the city.

The official response, when it came, was slow and confused, leaving tens of thousands of people without food, water, medical treatment or public services. Civil disorder developed, with reports of looting and violence, and poor coordination among public officials.

Better Planning Equals Fewer Costs

With better planning, hundreds of deaths could have been avoided and billions of dollars in property and productivity could have been preserved. Better planning could also have greatly reduced the fear, discomfort, frustration and violence experienced by residents.

Periodical and Internet Sources Bibliography

The following articles have been selected to supplement the diverse views presented in this chapter.

Christie Bacal	"Building Resilience to Disaster in One of the World's 'Most Disaster-Prone Countries,'" International Organization for Migration, January 29, 2013. www.iom.int.
Olga Belogolova	"Offshore Drilling Reform Not on the Horizon," *National Journal*, May 24, 2011.
Christopher Dickey	"Time to Brace for the Next 9/11," *Newsweek*, September 4, 2011.
Economist	"Cyber-Security: War on Terabytes," February 2, 2013.
Kristalina Georgieva	"Raising Our Game on Disaster Preparedness and Response," European Commission, November 15, 2012. http://europa.eu.
Alex Hannaford	"The Rock That Could Take Us Back to the Stone Age," *Sunday Telegraph*, October 30, 2011.
IRIN	"Uganda: Learning Lessons from Lethal Landslides," June 27, 2012. www.irinnews.org.
Melanie D.G. Kaplan	"Why Americans Aren't Prepared for the Next Mega Disaster," SmartPlanet, July 14, 2010. www.smartplanet.com.
Stephen A. Nelson	"Natural Disasters & Assessing Hazards and Risk," August 20, 2013. www.tulane.edu /~sanelson/Natural_Disasters/introduction.htm.
Mrigank Tiwari	"Stampede Not in Railway's Disaster Management Plan: Expert," *Times of India*, February 12, 2013.

GLOBALVIEWPOINTS

CHAPTER 4

Disaster Response and Aftermath

Disease Often Follows Natural Disasters

CBC News

In the following viewpoint, writers from the Canadian Broadcasting Corporation (CBC) discuss the likelihood of diseases following a natural disaster. They argue that most cases of disease derive from crowded conditions, unsafe water, contamination of food, and poor sanitation. They list cholera as the most dangerous of the diseases but also describe other dangerous infections, including dysentery and hepatitis. In addition, animal and insect bites can spread diseases in the wake of a disaster. Finally, the writers debunk the myth that corpses spread diseases, stating the risk of unburied corpses is negligible.

As you read, consider the following questions:

1. How many people are affected yearly by typhoid fever, according to the viewpoint?
2. Under what conditions does CBC News say balantidiasis is most commonly spread?
3. What do unfounded concerns about the infectiousness of corpses lead to, according to the viewpoint?

Long after the immediate threat passes, a natural disaster can continue to take a deadly toll.

Outbreaks of infectious diseases following hurricanes, cyclones, floods, tsunamis and earthquakes are not uncommon in the developing world. They are rare in developed countries.

Most post-disaster disease is spawned by poor sanitation, a lack of safe drinking water and contaminated food.

The Canadian Forces' Disaster Assistance Response Team has been dispatched to several natural disasters—in part—to help provide safe drinking water and reduce the risk of disease outbreak.

Here's a rundown of some of the diseases that can afflict survivors of disasters.

Cholera Is a Serious Post-Disaster Risk

Cholera is an intestinal infection caused by the bacterium *Vibrio cholerae*. People contract it from drinking contaminated water or eating contaminated food. It may be the biggest disease threat to survivors of disasters because it progresses rapidly. It can kill an individual in less than a day.

The infection leads to severe diarrhea—leading to the loss of up to 10 litres [338 ounces] of bodily fluids in a day. That causes rapid dehydration, shock and the risk of death.

However, most people who become infected don't get sick. The vast majority of people who do show symptoms will develop mild or moderate cases of the disease. Those cases are often indistinguishable from other types of acute diarrhea.

Typhoid Fever Is Also a Threat

Typhoid fever is caused by the bacterium *Salmonella Typhi*. You get it by eating food or drinking fluids handled by an infected person. You can also get it if sewage contaminated with *Salmonella Typhi* bacteria gets into the water you use for drinking or washing.

The illness is uncommon in the developed world—most North American cases involve people who have travelled to developing countries.

Typhoid fever affects about 21.5 million people a year.

Symptoms of the disease include sustained high fever of 39°C to 40°C, a feeling of weakness, stomach pains, headache, or loss of appetite. Some people suffer from diarrhea. Others develop constipation. In some cases, patients develop a rash of flat, rose-coloured spots.

Among the most serious complications are intestinal bleeding or perforations.

The disease is treatable with antibiotics and there is a vaccine that can protect people. But for those trying to cope with a natural disaster in less developed parts of the world, a lack of access to treatment increases the risk that the complications may prove fatal.

[Cholera] may be the biggest disease threat to survivors of disasters because it progresses rapidly. It can kill an individual in less than a day.

Dysentery Is Dangerous

This [dysentery] is yet another disease that can be spread through contaminated drinking water, although it can also be caused by a parasite living in one's gut. The vast majority of cases are caused by bacteria.

Dysentery results in diarrhea in which there is blood and pus. In rare cases, it can kill individuals within 24 hours.

However, most cases clear up on their own, without treatment.

The main symptom is frequent, near-liquid diarrhea flecked with blood, mucus or pus. Other symptoms include:

• Sudden onset of high fever and chills.

- Abdominal pain.

- Cramps, bloating and flatulence.

- Urgent need to pass stool.

- A feeling that you still have to go.

- A loss of appetite.

- Headache and fatigue.

- Vomiting and dehydration.

If dehydration becomes severe, an infected person could be at risk of coma or death.

Dysentery is treated through rehydration and antibiotics.

Diseases such as infectious hepatitis, gastroenteritis, measles and tuberculosis could catch up with victims of a catastrophe stuck in a crowded shelter with insufficient sanitary facilities.

Additional Serious Post-Disaster Diseases

Hepatitis A and E. These diseases spread under unsanitary conditions, through human feces. People catch the virus by taking in contaminated water or food.

No specific treatment or antibiotic drug exists for either hepatitis A or E. Those suffering are urged to rest, stay hydrated and try to eat nutritious foods.

Balantidiasis. This condition—another gut-wrenching infection—is also caused by coming into contact with contaminated water. It is more commonly spread in areas where people and pigs live in close proximity.

Many pigs carry the bacteria that cause balantidiasis and it can be passed from pigs to humans. It can also be spread when pig feces get into water humans use for washing or drinking.

Risk Factors and Communicable Diseases After Natural Disasters

Major risk factors following natural disasters	Water-borne diseases			Airborne/droplet diseases				Vector-borne diseases		Injury/wound		Clinical phase of natural disasters		
	Diarrhea (cholera; dysentery)	Leptospirosis	Hepatitis	ARI (pneumonia/influenza)	Measles	Meningococcal meningitis	Tuberculosis	Malaria	Dengue fever	Tetanus	Cutaneous mucormycosis	Impact phase (0–4 days)	Postimpact phase (4 days–4 weeks)	Recovery phase (> 4 weeks)
Population displacement from nonendemic to endemic areas								√	√					√
Overcrowding (close and multiple contacts)	√			√	√	√	√						√	
Stagnant water after flood and heavy rains	√	√						√	√					√
Insufficient/contaminated water and poor sanitation conditions	√		√										√	
High exposure and proliferation to disease vectors		√						√	√					
Insufficient nutrient intake/malnutrition	√			√	√		√							√
Low vaccination coverage					√									
Injuries										√	√		√	√

TAKEN FROM: "Preventing and Controlling Infectious Diseases after Natural Disasters," United Nations University, March 13, 2012.

There have been outbreaks of balantidiasis in areas struck by typhoons. Symptoms of the condition include chronic diarrhea, occasional dysentery, nausea, foul breath, colitis, abdominal pain, weight loss, deep intestinal ulcerations and possibly perforation of the intestine. Left untreated, it can kill. However, in most cases, people with the condition show no symptoms.

Leptospirosis Contaminated drinking water can bring on yet another condition—leptospirosis. You're at risk when water is contaminated by the urine of animals that carry the bacteria that causes leptospirosis—cattle, pigs, horses, dogs, rodents and wild animals.

Symptoms include high fever, severe headache, chills, muscle aches and vomiting. Those infected can also develop jaundice, red eyes, abdominal pain, diarrhea, or a rash.

If left untreated, the patient could develop kidney damage, meningitis, liver failure and respiratory distress. In rare cases, leptospirosis can kill.

It can be treated through antibiotics.

There was an outbreak of the disease in 1996 in Puerto Rico in the aftermath of a hurricane.

Animals and Insects Pose Threats

You may not be the only one competing for safe spaces in the wake of a natural disaster. Creepy, crawly creatures could be on the move as well if their breeding sites or natural habitats are ravaged.

The decaying body of a previously healthy person is not a disease risk.

If you're in a tropical country, you may be at increased risk of bites from poisonous spiders and snakes. As well, mosquitoes may become more of a threat, if they've been forced to move on to other breeding grounds.

You could be at risk for:

- *Malaria*—an infectious disease spread by mosquitoes, mainly in tropical climates. Symptoms, which begin showing up 10 to 15 days after infection, include headache and fever, chills, muscle and joint pain, nausea and vomiting and convulsions. If not treated promptly, you could die.

- *Dengue fever*—another infectious disease spread by mosquitoes. Symptoms include sudden onset of fever, with severe headache, muscle and joint pains and rashes. Cases often clear up within six to seven days. However, in severe cases, death can result.

For those who survived the disaster but lost their homes and had to seek shelter in an emergency centre, there are additional risks. Diseases such as infectious hepatitis, gastroenteritis, measles and tuberculosis could catch up with victims of a catastrophe stuck in a crowded shelter with insufficient sanitary facilities. This can be compounded in countries where immunization rates are low.

Corpses Are Not Harmful

In major disasters, there may be a large number of unburied corpses. In a natural disaster, the vast majority of those people were killed by the trauma of the storm—not disease. While the decomposing bodies will give off a terrible smell, they will not spread epidemic infectious diseases. The decaying body of a previously healthy person is not a disease risk.

A study published in the May 2004 edition of the *Pan American Journal of Public Health* found that the risk of epidemics from the bodies of people killed in natural disasters is negligible. The researchers found that epidemics resulting in mass fatalities after natural disasters have only occurred from a few diseases—such as cholera, typhoid, tuberculosis, anthrax and smallpox. While those diseases can be highly contagious, they cannot survive for long in dead bodies. The study found that survivors are far more likely to spread disease than corpses.

The researchers noted that unfounded concerns about the infectiousness of corpses sometimes leads to the rapid, unplanned disposal of the dead—often before victims are identified, making it harder for survivors to mourn their loss.

The Aftermath of the Japanese Tsunami Triggers a Potential United States Environmental Disaster

Becky Bohrer

In the following viewpoint, Becky Bohrer writes about projections concerning the debris created by the Japanese earthquake and tsunami of March 11, 2011. Many scientists believe that much of the debris will wash up on the shores of the western United States, creating an environmental disaster. According to Bohrer, little funding has been earmarked for the cleanup, and there is no comprehensive plan as to how to respond to the debris, leading to further worries about its impact. Bohrer is the Associated Press's political and statehouse reporter in Juneau, Alaska.

As you read, consider the following questions:

1. What is the Japanese government's estimate of the number of tons of floating debris caused by the March 11, 2011, earthquake and tsunami, according to Bohrer?

2. How much funding has been allocated to clean up tsunami debris in the United States, according to the viewpoint?

Becky Bohrer, "Japan Tsunami Debris: US Braces for 'Environmental Disaster,'" *Huff-Post Green*, June 8, 2012. Reproduced by permission.

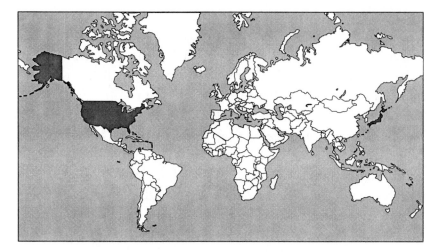

3. Who is Merrick Burden, and what does he think should happen regarding the debris, according to the viewpoint?

More than a year after a tsunami devastated Japan [in 2011], killing thousands of people and washing millions of tons of debris into the Pacific Ocean, the U.S. government and West Coast states don't have a cohesive plan for cleaning up the rubble that floats to American shores.

There is also no firm handle yet on just what to expect.

The Japanese government estimates that 1.5 million tons of debris is floating in the ocean from the catastrophe. Some experts in the United States think the bulk of that trash will never reach shore, while others fear a massive, slowly unfolding environmental disaster.

An Environmental Disaster in the Making

"I think this is far worse than any oil spill that we've ever faced on the West Coast or any other environmental disaster we've faced on the West Coast" in terms of the debris's weight, type and geographic scope, said Chris Pallister, president of a group dedicated to cleaning marine debris from the Alaska coastline.

David Kennedy, assistant administrator for the National Oceanic and Atmospheric Administration's [NOAA's] National Ocean Service, told a U.S. Senate panel last month [May 2012] that in most cases debris removal decisions will fall to individual states. Funding hasn't been determined.

U.S. Sen. Mark Begich, D [Democrat]-Alaska, and other West Coast political leaders, have called that scenario unacceptable, saying tsunami debris poses a pending national emergency. "If this was a one-time event all at once, we'd declare it an emergency and we'd be on the ground like that," he said, during the hearing he led.

One astonishing example of how the unexpected can suddenly appear occurred Wednesday in Oregon when a concrete and metal dock that measured 66 feet long, seven feet tall and 19 feet wide, washed ashore a mile north of Newport. A Japanese consulate official in Portland confirmed that the dock came from the northern Japanese city of Misawa, cut loose in the tsunami of March 11, 2011.

Some experts in the United States think the bulk [of the Japanese tsunami debris] will never reach shore, while others fear a massive, slowly unfolding environmental disaster.

"I think that the dock is a forerunner of all the heavier stuff that's coming later, and amongst that heavier stuff are going to be a lot of drums full of chemicals that we won't be able to identify," Pallister said.

His group, Gulf of Alaska Keeper, works in the same region devastated by the *Exxon Valdez* oil spill, which dumped 11 million gallons of oil into Prince William Sound in 1989.

Tsunami debris is tough to monitor. Winds and ocean currents regularly change, while rubbish can break up. Some trash, like fishing gear, kerosene and gas containers and building supplies, can be tied to the tsunami only anecdotally. But in other cases—a soccer ball and a derelict fishing boat in Alaska and a motorcycle in British Columbia, for example—items have been traced back to the disaster through their owners.

NOAA projects the debris having spread over an area roughly three times the size of the contiguous United States, but can't pinpoint when or how much might eventually reach the coasts of Alaska, Washington, Oregon, California and Hawaii.

An independent group of scientists and environmental activists are scheduled to sail aboard the *Sea Dragon* from Japan Saturday to an area north of the Hawaiian islands, with plans to zigzag through the debris, document what's floating and try to determine what might reach the West Coast.

"You have a unique experiment," said Marcus Eriksen, a researcher at the Algalita Marine Research Institute in Long Beach, Calif., who is leading the expedition. "You have entire homes and all their contents . . . anything you may find in a Japanese home could be floating in the ocean still intact."

Seattle-based oceanographer Curtis Ebbesmeyer, who has been tracking ocean trash for 20 years, predicts the main mass of tsunami debris will reach the U.S. coast from northern California to southeast Alaska as early as October, with the beginning of fall storms.

Cleanup plans should be finalized no later than September, Ebbesmeyer cautioned. There may also be sensitive issues to be decided, he said, including how to deal with any human remains or personal mementos.

Who Will Pay for the Cleanup Is Unknown

But just who will clean up the debris and who will pay for it hasn't been fully determined.

The Debris That Floated Away

Among the most visually stunning and disturbing images of the Japan tsunami were those showing the sheer volume of debris being swept up by returning waves and pulled out to sea. Such was the power of the tsunami that the debris included fishing boats, entire houses and everything in between. Large numbers of cars could also be seen floating in coastal waters. Within days of the tsunami, the patches of disaster debris floating off Japan's coast were so large they were visible on satellite images. . . .

The masses of floating debris have since spread to a much larger area, aided by wind and currents. There are numerous mathematical ocean current–based models which predict that these patches of marine debris will eventually be washed over onto the west coast of North America and also onto South Pacific islands. It is already known that the debris is no longer moving in single or multiple spectacular patches and is unlikely to arrive on any coastline in a sudden and dramatic fashion.

Both the US Environmental Protection Agency and US National Oceanic and Atmospheric Administration (NOAA) have been proactively looking for any signs of the debris arriving on US shores, as have the Canadian authorities. The US authorities have also committed to collect and return to Japan any debris which is clearly identifiable as being of Japanese origin and that may have sentimental value. As of early May 2012, debris suspected to be from the tsunami had washed up on the coastline of Alaska and Washington State, among other areas, and was being documented.

United Nations Environment Programme,
"Managing Post-Disaster Debris: The Japan Experience," June 2012,
pp. 41–2. www.unep.org/pdf/UNEP_Japan_post-tsunami_debris.pdf.

Begich wants to make at least $45 million available for local community groups to conduct cleanup efforts. Gulf of Alaska Keeper believes Congress should set aside $50 million a year for four years.

As it stands now, NOAA has $618,000 allocated to clean up tsunami debris. The agency's total marine debris program budget could drop by 26 percent to $3.4 million, under President [Barack] Obama's proposed budget.

Marine trash isn't a new problem. The ocean is littered with all kinds of things that can trap and kill wildlife, hurt human health and navigation and blight beaches.

NOAA has previously given grants to local groups for cleanup work. The agency expects the tsunami debris to simply add to the ongoing problem of massive amounts of trash flowing into the ocean every day.

[The National Oceanic and Atmospheric Administration] projects the debris having spread over an area roughly three times the size of the contiguous United States.

Volunteers in California report their efforts being stretched thin just in dealing with day-to-day rubbish. Seasonal opportunity for cleanup could close as early as September at spots in Alaska, where some beaches are accessible only by boat or aircraft and removing trash can be difficult and expensive. Washington has monitored some incoming debris for radioactivity.

Eben Schwartz, marine debris program manager for the California Coastal Commission, said more recognition needs to be given to the fact that it will be beach cleanup volunteers who respond to tsunami debris.

"Given that, I would like to see more state and federal support for the volunteer programs that will be taking the lead," he said. They're going to need help, resources and funding, he said.

NOAA's marine debris program expects solid plans from the states within the next few months. The governors of Washington, Oregon and California, as well as the premier of British Columbia, have said they will work together to manage debris.

Widespread or concentrated die-offs of marine animals aren't expected, said John Hocevar, oceans campaign director for Greenpeace, but there could be local impacts.

NOAA officials say they don't think there's any radiation risk from the debris, despite the meltdown at a nuclear power plant in Fukushima.

Merrick Burden, executive director of the Marine Conservation Alliance in Alaska and Washington, said he thinks states, local governments, volunteers and industries including fishing and tourism need to pull together to clean up debris, and not simply wait and hope for federal funds.

"One of the things standing in the way is a unified, coordinated approach to this," he said.

Pallister worried that a lack of awareness may hamper the effort.

"You just don't have that visceral, gut-wrenching reaction to having oiled otters and drowned seabirds in that crude to get the public pumped up about it," he said of the tsunami debris. "And even if you could get the public pumped up, again, you don't have that culprit to go after—a bad guy. It's kind of a tough one to deal with."

Britain Proposes a New Way of Responding to Disasters

Rachel Sylvester and Alice Thomson

In the following viewpoint, Rachel Sylvester and Alice Thomson interview British diplomat Lord Paddy Ashdown concerning his report evaluating British response to worldwide humanitarian disasters. Lord Ashdown believes Britain must seriously change the way it offers aid and opines that the world is a far more dangerous place now than in the past. The need for emergency response will only grow in the future, and Britain must be prepared. Sylvester is a British political journalist. Thomson is an associate editor of the London Times.

As you read, consider the following questions:

1. To where did Prime Minister David Cameron invite Lord Ashdown, according to the viewpoint?
2. On what grounds do the authors say the Liberal Democrats opposed the war in Iraq?
3. How old is Lord Ashdown, according to the viewpoint?

Paddy Ashdown has always been Westminster's Action Man. He prefers submarines to helicopters: "I used to swim in and out of them under water when I was in the Special Boat

Rachel Sylvester and Alice Thomson, "Why Britain Needs a New Way of Responding to a Disastrous World; Saturday Interview," *The Times*, March 26, 2011, pp. 36–37. Reproduced by permission.

Service," he tells us. He favours the jungle to the desert—"I feel more at home there"—but will not divulge how many men he has killed with his bare hands. "Mind your own business," he says when we ask.

As MP [member of Parliament] for Yeovil, he led the Liberal charge into Conservative territory in the West Country. As Liberal Democrat leader he almost did a deal with [former prime minister] Tony Blair to form a coalition with Labour. As Lord Ashdown of Norton sub Hamdon, he was sent to sort out Bosnia as international high representative. When he was appointed to investigate parades in Northern Ireland, where he had served as a young Marine, he found himself negotiating with the former IRA [Irish Republican Army] commander who had put him on a death list.

The fluent Mandarin speaker is now the éminence grise [powerful decision maker] of the coalition. [British Prime Minister] David Cameron invited him to a Chequers [county residence of the prime minister] summit on Afghanistan and [Deputy Prime Minister] Nick Clegg relies on him for political advice. "If the elected government of the day asks me to do something, then I do it if I can," Lord Ashdown says.

Disaster Relief Must Be Changed

On Monday [March 28, 2011,] the report of his Humanitarian Emergency Response Review will be published. With floods in Pakistan and Australia, earthquakes in Haiti and New Zealand, a tsunami in Japan and a possible refugee crisis in Libya, it could not be better timed.

He says that there is a "perfect storm" of climate change, population rise, economic crisis, food shortages, increased seismic activity and political upheaval that is making the world more dangerous than ever. "The number of natural disasters is going up. They are not an aberration, it is a growing trend. We are going to have to change our way of looking at disaster relief."

His report predicts that 375 million people will be affected by climate-related disasters by 2015, up from 263 million last year. "The world is more interconnected than it has ever been. We are living in extremely turbulent times. We are also seeing massive shifts in power. Events are gathering pace." Britain must focus "on how to get through these times in the best possible shape".

There is a "perfect storm" of climate change, population rise, economic crisis, food shortages, increased seismic activity and political upheaval making the world more dangerous than ever.

Thirty years ago, a defence secretary had to worry only about having the best army, navy and air force. Now, "if I were defence minister I would have to talk to the Minister of Health about pandemics, the Department of Agriculture about food shortages, the Minister of Industry about the fragility of our high-tech infrastructure and the Home Office about immigration."

The Department for International Development [DfID] must change too. "In the past, DfID has had a tendency to be a little too muscular. We like that spirit but now it needs to build more alliances with countries like China."

It is the only department that has been ring-fenced from spending cuts, but as the big-squeeze budget takes effect, will people mind giving so much to good causes abroad? "My guess is that people are happy to help for a humanitarian crisis but for day-to-day aid they are less sure. The ring-fence puts the onus on us to be accountable and give good value for money."

Does that include helping rich countries such as Japan if they have a humanitarian crisis? "They haven't asked for money but if they do we should consider it. The search-and-rescue people dashed out there but I don't think they checked and I am not sure they were wanted."

His report concludes that there should be a shift towards giving "cash rather than blankets" to disaster victims. "If you give money directly to people they go to the market and buy things, so you stimulate economic activity. It helps to create independence rather than dependency."

There must be better co-ordination between non-governmental agencies [or organisations] (NGOs). "In Haiti there were something like 1,400 NGOs. When I was in Bosnia, it became NGO city. There's a real problem."

The United Nations Is a Problem

The biggest stumbling block to emergency assistance is, in his view, the United Nations [UN], which is putting lives at risk. "The international leadership in Haiti and Pakistan was an absolute shambles. The problem is that whoever happens to be the resident coordinator carries on when there has been a massive disaster. Suddenly there is the US fleet outside, billions of pounds coming in and the person isn't equipped to deal with that."

Lord Ashdown, who is president of Unicef UK [the United Nations Children's Fund, United Kingdom], wants the UN secretary-general to create a specialist emergencies team. "We are wasting lives and we are wasting money at present."

Perhaps the UN has passed its sell-by date. "We need a forum for international matters but the UN is an appalling manager of executive action and of what happens post-conflict. In Bosnia the 'coalition of the willing' was responsive to all my needs as high representative. But my neighbour in Kosovo who was the UN special representative wasn't given the backing he needed." The UN should "subcontract" military intervention "to an organisation that is capable of fighting wars" and concentrate on being a "legitimiser of international action".

[Lord Ashdown's] report concludes that there should be a shift towards giving "cash rather than blankets" to disaster victims.

The Liberal Democrats opposed the Iraq war on the ground that it was not legitimised by the UN. It was, he says, "absolutely essential" to have UN backing for military action in Libya. "Barack Obama has been greatly criticised for taking a back seat but he has handled this extremely well. He knows that America has become a toxic brand so he is creating space for others to come in."

The West will never again be able to act as a "cowboy posse" strutting around the world. "Iraq and Afghanistan were the last of the old wars, when the West could get together and dispose of regimes on their own. Now you have to look further, involve the Arabs and the Chinese. We now have to think about uncomfortable coalitions with people with whom we don't share values but we may share interests."

The key to the crisis in Libya is holding the international coalition together. "To do that we have to maintain legality." There are already conflicting messages about whether trying to topple Colonel Muammar Gaddafi is the ultimate goal. "If

Mr Gaddafi is confused about whether we want to target him, then I'm entirely in favour of that. I don't think it is part of our job to help him sleep more soundly at night." But is it legal to assassinate the Libyan leader? "My guess is it probably isn't in these circumstances. But if Gaddafi started acting differently then you want to maintain the flexibility to be able to do it."

Considering the Japanese Nuclear Crisis

The international community is dealing with two crises at the same time. Lord Ashdown says that Britain must think through the implications of the nuclear crisis in Japan. He had been a recent convert to nuclear power but now he says: "What you see before you is a person whose judgment about this has been seriously shaken by what's gone on. I think that as a politician, like as a soldier, you have to be prepared to take risks from time to time and I was wondering whether this was a risk we would have to consider in order to stop the world frying.

"I have concluded that what has happened in Japan makes this proposition unsellable. I think Japan has changed the public's mind."

This country may not be vulnerable to earthquakes and tsunamis but he warns: "If you don't live on a fault line you've still got other problems which would create instability—terrorist attack is one, having a war is another. Somebody could drop a bomb on a nuclear power station. Are we really prepared to have an energy system that depends on not having a war for 1,000 years?" People must find other ways to create and to save energy. "All governments are going to have to address issues which nuclear power helped them to dodge. One of those is altering the way we live our lives."

Many senior Liberal Democrats share his concerns about nuclear power, which was one of the main areas of disagreement with the Conservatives when the coalition was formed.

Changes in British Emergency Response

The last year [until mid-2011] has seen an unprecedented number of disasters, from the massive floods in Pakistan to the shocking death and destruction caused by the earthquake and tsunami in Japan. Meanwhile the long-term suffering caused by conflict in countries such as Sudan and the Democratic Republic of [the] Congo continues, even as new conflict brings fresh misery and oppression in Libya.

Lord [Paddy] Ashdown's timely review of the way the UK [United Kingdom] delivers humanitarian assistance identifies much the British public can be proud of. My department, the Department for International Development, is praised for its leading role in international efforts. But Lord Ashdown also highlights the daunting challenges we face, and calls for us to respond now in order to be ready. . . .

And I am determined that we seize this moment. We cannot just 'enhance the status quo'. Many millions will suffer if we collectively fail this challenge, and fragile development gains will be lost. The Humanitarian Emergency Response Review, properly implemented, will help us make the changes needed and we will live up to its ambition both in spirit and in the detail.

To deliver this change, we must be clear that our starting point is in our collective humanity. The British people are amongst the most generous in times of international disaster, rising above national interest or allegiance. The government is committed that our humanitarian aid must continue to be delivered on the basis of need and need alone.

Andrew Mitchell, "Foreword,"
Humanitarian Emergency Response Review: UK Government
Response, *Department for International Development, June 2011.*

Lord Ashdown says that Mr Cameron and Mr Clegg are good at resolving difficult issues. "Each leader has a different style. Cameron is a chairman type—he sees himself as being the gatherer of opinions. Nick, as the leader of the smaller party, has to have a greater clarity about where he's going.

"They are different but not as different as Barack Obama and George Bush, or Tony Blair and Gordon Brown. They both deal with things in a rational fashion, uncluttered by prejudice or preconceived views."

The Liberal Democrats must have a "clear identity" at the next election. But the man who insisted on standing halfway between Labour and the Tories [political parties] says: "I don't want to go back to using the word 'equidistant' because the world has changed." He predicts that Labour will look increasingly like "a bunch of superannuated students shouting from the sidelines".

"If you don't live on a fault line you've still got other problems which would create instability. . . . Somebody could drop a bomb on a nuclear power station."

Holding the Coalition Together

A "no" vote in the alternative vote referendum would make him "bloody miserable" but it would not, in his view, break the coalition. More dangerous are the cracks that have appeared over the NHS [National Health Service]. "If someone asks me, as a liberal, would I prefer to put power in the hands of practitioners rather than bureaucrats, my answer is yes, but when you are dealing with these highly complex mechanisms such as health, education or welfare, which are festooned with the laws of unintended consequences, the policy should be festina lente [make haste slowly]."

Lord Ashdown is convinced that the coalition will last another four years. "There's amity—not love—and a sense of partnership which I have found surprising. It would be much worse for us if the coalition didn't exist. I'm immensely proud that I was the founding leader of a party that didn't collapse and is now a party of government."

So would he take a ministerial job? "I'm very content with my life. I'm really not interested. I do not seek it, I do not desire it. I'm 70, I've got plenty to get on with in the garden."

But it is unlikely that he will retire quite yet.

The World Bank Responds Effectively to the Haiti Earthquake

Independent Evaluation Group

In the following viewpoint, the Independent Evaluation Group (IEG), charged with assessing the actions taken by the World Bank, details the response of the World Bank to the 2010 earthquake in Haiti. The IEG asserts that experience with previous disasters made the World Bank's response in Haiti especially effective, due to the lessons learned. Among these, according to the viewpoint, are early involvement; the understanding that each decision affects all that follows; and that employment and cash early in the recovery are important for survivors. Haiti's situation was especially difficult due to the huge death toll and the extreme poverty of the country.

As you read, consider the following questions:

1. What is the tendency of people immediately after an earthquake, according to the viewpoint?

2. In what countries does IEG assert large multifamily spaces serving as temporary disaster shelters have led to social breakdown?

Independent Evaluation Group, "The World Bank Group Response to the Haiti Earthquake: Evaluative Lessons," *Evaluation Brief 10*, 2011, pp. 1–7. Creative Commons Attribution CC BY 3.0.

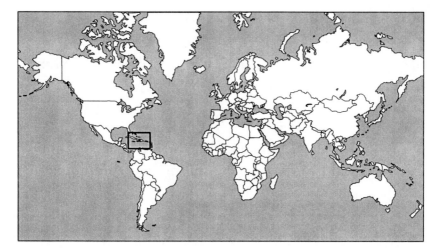

3. What are some of the questions that are new and special to Haiti with regard to recovering from the earthquake, according to the viewpoint?

As Haiti faces the daunting task of recovery after the devastating [2010] earthquake, past experiences provide some lessons. Factors making a crucial difference to the effectiveness of actions include the nature of the immediate response, diagnosis, project design and supervision, use of local capacity, private sector links, and coordination among partners, including within the World Bank Group. Many of the lessons from previous natural disaster episodes are relevant now; yet, Haiti's distinct country conditions must also be kept in mind.

Indeed, several factors make the response in Haiti especially overwhelming—the breakdown of social order and a fragile security situation; the near-complete loss of governance structures; and the failure, before the earthquake, to impose even minimum quality standards on the construction industry. Complicating matters further will be the unprecedented scale of charitable donations earmarked for emergency relief, and the arrival of many new relief agencies, which tend to prioritize unilateral action over coordination.

Early World Bank Involvement Is Essential

The [1999] Marmara earthquake experience in Turkey shows the merit of early World Bank Group involvement. Consultative groups have been effective in mobilizing aid resources and facilitating coordination in post-conflict situations. One disaster-experienced country director suggests that consultative groups could also be useful in coordinating aid disaster operations, which proved successful in Sudan in putting together a multi-donor famine effort.

Front-end preparation—including joint damage and needs assessments before consultative group meetings—should be agreed on before operations are put into place. Identifying local leadership and project management offices is particularly important. When credible physical, economic, and social assessments are available, countries ultimately mobilize more assistance than otherwise.

Because capacity to use aid effectively in fragile states is low and governance is often poor, the focus from the beginning also needs to be on the development of capacity and the improvement of governance, not merely the reconstruction of physical infrastructure.

Early actions have a major impact on the recovery. How relief distributions are managed either enhances reconstruction or constrains it. It is far more difficult to stop the use of force and firearms, looting, and rioting than it is to prevent such actions in the first place. The tendency of people immediately after an earthquake is to band together to recover survivors from fallen buildings. Ensuring and maintaining mutual trust is important for effective reconstruction efforts. The rebuilding of homes and communities requires the safe transportation and storage of building materials; often, community groups need to be formed, to work together in rebuilding homes and infrastructure. Since early actions influence project success, World Bank Group staff need to realize the importance of early actions and advise development partners accordingly.

Social Relationships Must Be Preserved

If possible, avoid expensive temporary shelter under a [World] Bank project. People are able to find adequate temporary shelter using materials from damaged buildings, and families that did not lose their dwellings will help shelter friends and relatives (as occurred in Colombia after the Armero eruption [of the stratovolcano Nevado del Ruiz], and in Grenada and St. Lucia after Hurricane Ivan). Relief efforts usually spend more on tents and temporary shelter than the amounts ultimately made available for permanent housing. If people are moved out of the main cities and shelters are required, serious efforts need to be made to keep families and neighborhood groupings intact for reasons of social support and continuity.

Early actions have a major impact on the recovery [from a disaster].

The physical layout of temporary shelter structures can help reduce crime and violence against women if care is taken during the relocation process to ensure that as many doors of the shelter, as possible, face a common and well-lit area. Such a layout avoids the creation of dark passages and alleyways, which are not in clear view and are potential places for assaults to occur. Also, large, shared, multifamily spaces have led to social breakdown in Colombia (Armero), Mexico City, and Turkey.

Paid Work for Survivors Helps

The general population can be helped to recover emotionally through the rebuilding process with paid work (as was done in Gujarat [India]). Taking the time to ensure that all usable building materials are recovered and recycled is a way to ensure that the poor will be able to afford to rebuild. Once work opportunities associated with clearing rubble and recycling materials diminish, it is important to provide cash assistance targeted at families (as in the aftermath of the Marmara earthquake).

Cash transfers are more important than providing food, blankets, and clothing. Indeed, in most disasters, sending canned food and used clothing from overseas is counterproductive. For example, in Bangladesh following a major cyclone, imported food aid destroyed the local rice market. With cash transfers, the distribution of emergency supplies is more orderly, involves local leadership, and helps to enhance social cohesion.

Simple Damage Assessment Is Necessary

Safety evaluations of buildings after an earthquake should determine if structures are inhabitable. If they are not, a plan for the displaced occupants needs to be prepared. In Haiti, project design will need to take into account the fact that there is diminished functional capacity at the local, national, and community levels. Alternative networks, such as nongovernmental organizations and the United Nations agencies, can fill gaps in capacity, but their participation should be coupled with a plan to rebuild government administrative capacity.

Following the Maharashtra [India] earthquake, the damage assessment was based on a complicated compensation system. The use of criteria from the International Association of Earthquake Engineering for damage assessment of individual housing units, in this situation, proved to be difficult because the criteria for modern, engineered housing do not work for mud-bonded or stacked-stone structures. When people are compensated in variable amounts for the actual damage to their homes, they will appeal the decisions and argue with the compensators; they may even inflict more damage on their homes to receive more money. In contrast, if people are paid set amounts for easily determined levels of damage, as occurred in Gujarat, there is then no opportunity for further negotiation.

Donor coordination has always proved to be vital. Ways must be found for involved donors to work together or in parallel, in the short term, on a clearly defined set of aid activities with the same eligibility requirements and benefits. . . .

Long-Term Vulnerability Must Be Reduced

The [World] Bank's Operational Policies have long called for natural disaster projects to reduce long-term vulnerability. In Haiti, the current perceived urgency of emergency and reconstruction tasks can be expected to lead to a loss of focus on mitigation/disaster risk reduction, in the face of many competing demands. Interestingly, the opposite situation, that is, the long time between earthquake occurrences, also works toward the same result. Disaster mitigation, because it is a periodic rather than a constant need, tends to lose out to other priorities—especially once the disaster recedes from international media attention and immediate relief needs have been met.

Cash transfers are more important than providing food, blankets, and clothing.

Reaching agreement on mitigation measures with the government, within the first three months, is important because it becomes harder to get politicians to focus on a disaster once the memory of the emergency fades. Outcomes are usually better if a financing mechanism for the agreed mitigation measures is defined and locked in. Options to consider include financial incentives, land use and management practices, a review of land tenure patterns, upgraded building codes, training for construction craftspeople, and other nonstructural measures to lessen vulnerability. . . .

Neighborhoods Should Be Preserved by All Those Involved

There is frequently pressure to relocate communities after a disaster. Relocation during post-earthquake reconstruction of settlements that consist mostly of one- and two-story buildings is usually a mistake because it is not all that difficult for local builders to make small buildings earthquake resistant. To take an example, in India it was believed that villages built on cotton soil needed to be relocated, which ultimately turned out to be wrong. Another example involves moving people away from coastal zones. The tendency for these residents to return is almost irresistible because of the economic advantages and other amenities associated with living by the sea.

In-situ reconstruction should be promoted after earthquakes, to take advantage of existing infrastructure and community facilities, while minimizing resettlement and social dislocation. Communities help themselves when low-cost reconstruction is done in-situ. It is common for outsiders and victims to clamor for relocation in the early days after a disaster but, with time, the importance of preserving social relationships institutionalized in the current neighborhood structures reasserts itself. Moreover, problems can be created by uneven incentives for rehabilitation, as compared with reconstruction. In India, villages litigated for the right to relocate, even when it was technically contraindicated, because the benefits given to families that only rehabilitated were far worse than the benefits given to relocated groups.

Bank emergency reconstruction lending used to expect cost recovery at levels that could not feasibly take place, given how much disaster victims had lost and needed to replace. Following the El Salvador earthquake, the [World] Bank project targeted low-income families and expected full cost recovery. An IEG [Independent Evaluation Group] evaluation later found that over half of the original beneficiaries had been unable to pay and had given up their homes.

However, when beneficiaries do not make any contribution, demands can become inflated and unreasonable. For example, the Maharashtra emergency project provided finished houses for free, but led to escalating expectations among beneficiaries. Beneficiaries became unwilling to pay user charges for urban services. One group made demands that the government paint and maintain their gift houses in perpetuity.

Natural disasters rip apart social cohesiveness. Rebuilding social structures is a large challenge.

A compromise with beneficiaries making a limited contribution seems to work best. For example, in the Argentina flood reconstruction project, beneficiaries of new housing had to make contributions in materials and labor.

During project design, staff often believe that the only way to produce the huge number of new dwellings is to bring in large contractors. In India, where people were given funds to repair their units, most of the families actually economized enough to build altogether new houses, and contractors were generally not involved. In those villages it was possible to use local people in the construction, so employment was created for people from the disaster-affected region. Contractors generally used imported labor to work 12–14 hours a day doing piecework.

Also, when homeowners were put in charge of the process, houses were better adapted to each family's needs; there was not a one-size-fits-all approach. The reliance on owner-managed construction was even more widely used following a subsequent earthquake in Gujarat, with equally positive results. Supervisory personnel did not always need higher education. Projects for post-disaster housing were effectively and economically supervised by builders and masons rather than engineers, at least as regards owner-built structures.

Social Structures Must Be Kept

The impacts of disasters on people vary, depending on the levels of social vulnerability and risk. The recovery process is potentially even more uneven, and it tends to be less visible. When the pressure of the immediate response carries over to the later stages, too little may be done to ensure that the social needs of the affected populations are considered. Natural disasters rip apart social cohesiveness. Rebuilding social structures is a large challenge and one that is rarely done well by any of the institutions, in large part because the character of the initial response makes doing so more difficult.

Earthquake disasters often strike informal or squatter settlements particularly hard. Responses need to take the plight of the renters and squatters into account so as not to increase social inequities. While earthquake-resistant building codes help those in the formal sector, such codes will never be applied in informal settlements and special measures are needed. . . .

Haiti's challenges are all the more daunting because of the enormous death toll and horrendous human suffering, and the sheer scale of destruction—not only of the physical infrastructure but also of the social fabric and the institutional setting. Crucial in the recovery will be not only the size of financing but also its quality and use. There are many useful lessons for effectiveness. Yet, many questions will also be new and special to Haiti—among them are how a multi-donor aid effort plays out, what quality of governance emerges during the reconstruction, what urban design emerges in the reconstruction, how post-disaster social networks are shaped, and how even such an enormous calamity might provide the chance for a new beginning.

The International Monetary Fund's Response Endangers Haiti's Recovery

Bretton Woods Project

In the following viewpoint, the Bretton Woods Project reveals that the International Monetary Fund's (IMF's) loans to Haiti after the 2010 earthquake place the country in excessive debt. Although some of the money owed to the IMF and World Bank has been cancelled or deferred, Haiti nonetheless continues to owe a large percentage of its gross domestic product to outside agencies. Thus, monies given to Haiti to aid in reconstruction could ultimately delay or prevent recovery, as so much of the country's resources will have to be used to service the debt rather than helping the people. The Bretton Woods Project is a World Bank and IMF watchdog agency.

As you read, consider the following questions:

1. What was Haiti's existing debt to the International Monetary Fund, including the new loan for earthquake recovery, at the end of January 2010?

2. For how many years did the World Bank suspend repayment of Haiti's $39 million debt?

"Debt Aftershocks to Shake Haiti's Recover?," Bretton Woods Project, February 12, 2010, p. 69. Reproduced by permission.

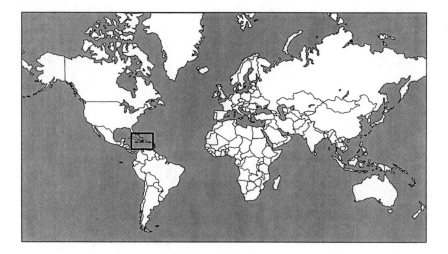

3. What does Benjamin Leo's research reveal, according to the viewpoint?

An IMF [International Monetary Fund] loan to Haiti in response to the devastating earthquake in early January [2010] has been criticised for exacerbating the country's debt burden and endangering recovery.

The IMF approved a loan of $102 million at the end of January, which, although interest free and subject to a five-and-a-half-year grace period, adds to Haiti's existing $166 million debt to the fund. The loan runs counter to earlier IMF warnings from the IMF that Haiti remains at high risk of debt distress and that "new borrowing policies must remain cautious."

In reaction to the financial crisis, the IMF made loans to all of its poorest borrowers, including Haiti, interest free from 2009 to 2012. However, when Haiti's payments resume, the IMF expects they will equate to 2.8 per cent of government revenues by 2014, in a country with an 80 per cent poverty rate.

The World Bank and International Monetary Fund Hurt Poor Countries

Here's a typical example of what happened [when the World Bank and International Monetary Fund (IMF) intervened]. In Malawi, the country's soil had become badly depleted, so the government decided to subsidise fertiliser for farmers. When the IMF and World Bank came in, they called this "a market distortion," and ordered Malawi to stop at once. They did. So the country's crops failed, and famine scythed through the population.

Johann Hari,
"There's Real Hope from Haiti and It's Not What You Expect,"
Independent, *February 5, 2010.*

Civil society network Jubilee South expressed its "demand that the resources allocated for relief and reconstruction do not create more debt, or conditionalities."

For its part, the World Bank made a grant of $100 million towards reconstruction and recovery, the cost of which could exceed $1 billion—15 per cent of Haiti's GDP [gross domestic product]—according to its preliminary estimates. The Haitian prime minister Jean-Max Bellerive voiced concern that the cost could be four times as much.

The bank also announced it would suspend repayment demands for Haiti's $39 million debt for five years. This amount is outstanding after almost half a billion dollars owed to the bank's International Development Association was cancelled last year [2009] as part of the Multilateral Debt Relief Initiative (MDRI). Prior to the earthquake, Haiti's total external debt stood at $1.25 billion, half what it was before a previous cancellation in 2009.

Dithering on Debt Cancellation

After facing fierce criticism from civil society that debt and conditionality had exacerbated Haiti's vulnerability by limiting the state's capacity to prepare for disasters, the bank and IMF joined a growing chorus advocating further debt cancellation. Bilateral creditors including the [international finance group] G7 countries and Venezuela announced they would cancel their share of the Haitian debt. Bowing to campaigners' pressure, the G7 finance ministers stated, "The debt to multilateral institutions should be forgiven and we'll work with these institutions and other partners to make this happen as soon as possible." Details remained vague however, and the IMF's director of external relations referred to debt relief for Haiti as a "medium-term issue." It is unclear whether cancellation will be financed from existing internal resources or with aid money from donors.

Camille Chalmers of the civil society network, Haitian Platform to Advocate Alternative Development, said, "The debts imposed by the IFIs [international financial institutions] and the major world powers have contributed to destroying our country. It's the equivalent of an earthquake which has lasted from late in 1983 when we signed the first stand-by agreement with the IMF. These loans have caused earthquakes, aftershocks and tremors that have undermined our institutions and our capacity to respond to a crisis of this magnitude."

New Global Debt Crisis

According to research by Benjamin Leo, a former US Treasury official, the World Bank's lending to the most indebted countries remains almost as high as before it introduced the Debt Sustainability Framework [for Low-Income Countries] in 2004 to avert debt problems. In a November 2009 paper for US think tank Center for Global Development, Leo argues that the international financial institutions determine a country's borrowing capacity on the basis of inadequate and volatile ratings. He warns that unsustainable debt has been further exacerbated by the IMF's emergency loans in response to the financial crisis. Leo calls for donors to "re-examine ... the system for determining the appropriate grant/loan mix", cautioning that without corrective action the international community could be forced into a further round of systematic debt cancellation.

"These loans have caused earthquakes, aftershocks and tremors that have undermined our institutions and our capacity to respond to a crisis of this magnitude."

Nick Dearden, director of UK NGO [United Kingdom nongovernmental organisation] the Jubilee Debt Campaign, concurred: "Haiti would not be in this position if it weren't for the serious flaws in the Heavily Indebted Poor Countries and MDRI debt cancellation schemes which mean that a country is guaranteed to run up new debt while it completes the debt cancellation process. In the case of Haiti, this is another example of recycling odious debts—run up by the [former president François] Duvalier regime."

Meanwhile Iceland may resist pressure to rapidly repay its creditors, despite the UK and Netherlands blocking EU [European Union] crisis funds, on which IMF disbursements depend, until repayment terms are agreed. Public pressure has led the president to set a referendum in early March on the repayment terms, an unprecedented move.

The rising debt crisis will strengthen calls for a proper arbitration mechanism for debts that compromise development or are illegitimate.

Rwanda Cuts Disaster Risk at the Site of a Potential Explosion

Xan Rice

In the following viewpoint, Xan Rice details the dangers posed by Lake Kivu in Rwanda, a lake that has huge amounts of dissolved carbon dioxide and methane in its waters. These gases can erupt in what is known as a limnic eruption, causing large numbers of deaths among the people who live on Lake Kivu's shores. Rwanda is addressing the risk by harvesting the gases to provide electric power to Rwanda's residents, thereby addressing a pressing energy need with an effective disaster prevention method. Rice is the Guardian's *East Africa correspondent.*

As you read, consider the following questions:

1. How much electricity is the state-owned Kibuye Power plant currently producing, according to the viewpoint?

2. What are the names of the two other known "exploding lakes" in the world?

3. What did US company ContourGlobal do in 2009, as Rice reports?

Xan Rice, "Rwanda Harnesses Volcanic Gases from Depths of Lake Kivu," *The Guardian*, August 16, 2010. Reproduced by permission.

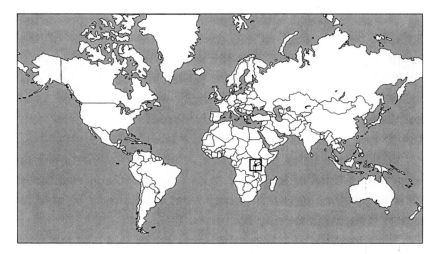

It's dusk on Lake Kivu and the fishermen sing while pad-dling out in their catamarans, three canoes secured together with long wooden poles. As the twin volcanoes on the far shore disappear into the darkness the men spark kerosene lamps to attract the sambaza sardines into their nets. Across the vast lake their lanterns offer the only tiny sequins of light.

Reducing Disaster Risk and Lighting Houses

At least that is how it used to be. Now, near the northern shore, the bright fluorescent bulbs illuminating a tall barge can be seen from miles away. It is the start of a project that could light up the whole of Rwanda for decades, while also reducing the risk of disaster for the two million people living alongside this rare "exploding lake".

In a world first, the barge is extracting gases that are trapped deep in Lake Kivu's waters like the fizz in a cham-pagne bottle. Methane, the main constituent of natural gas used for household cooking and heating, is then separated out and piped back to the rugged shore where it fires three large generators.

The state-owned Kibuye Power plant is already producing 3.6MW [megawatts] of electricity, more than 4% of the country's entire supply. But the success of the pilot project, and the huge unmet demand for power in Rwanda—only one in 14 homes has access to electricity—has encouraged local and foreign investors to commit hundreds of millions of dollars to new methane plants along the lakeshore.

Within two years [from 2010], the government hopes to be getting a third of its power from Lake Kivu, and eventually aims to produce so much energy from methane to be able to export it to neighbouring countries.

"Our grandfathers knew there was gas in this lake but now we have proved that it can be exploited," said Alexis Kabuto, the Rwandan engineer who runs the $20m [million] Kibuye project. "It's a cheap, clean resource that could last us 100 years."

A Killer Lake

Historically, Lake Kivu's gas has been a killer. Deaths attributed to invisible pockets of carbon dioxide rising from vents along the shoreline, known as mazukus, or "evil winds", are frequently reported, especially on the Congo side. But it is the gas dissolved in the water that may present a far greater threat.

Some scientists say that the ever-expanding volumes of carbon dioxide and methane in Lake Kivu, coupled with the nearby volcanic activity, make a limnic eruption (also referred to as a lake overturn, in which CO_2 suddenly erupts from the lake) highly likely at some stage in the future unless degassing occurs. This has now begun with the extraction of some of the 60bn cubic metres [about 2,118 billion cubic feet] of methane in the water.

The world's only two other known "exploding lakes", Monoun and Nyos, both in Cameroon, overturned in the 1980s. The clouds of carbon dioxide that burst through from the deep water left about 1,800 people dead from asphyxiation.

But Lake Kivu is nearly 2,000 times larger than Lake Nyos, and is in a far more densely populated area. Cindy Ebinger, a professor of earth sciences at the University of Rochester in the US, who co-authored a study earlier this year that described Kivu as possibly "one of the most dangerous lakes in the world", said: "You don't even want to think about the scale of the devastation that could occur."

The lake's potential to both enhance and destroy lives stems from its geography. Nestled on the border between Rwanda and Democratic Republic of [the] Congo, it sits at the highest point of the western arm of the Great Rift Valley. On the Congolese side, Mount Nyiragongo and Mount Nyamulagira have erupted in recent years, the former sending scalding tongues of lava into the lake in 2002. The seismic activity around the lake is responsible for the steady injection of volcanic gas into the water, where it settles in a dense saline layer more than 260 metres beneath the surface.

The ever-expanding volumes of carbon dioxide and methane in Lake Kivu ... make a limnic eruption ... highly likely.

Methane Harvesting Requires More Study

To harvest the methane, heavy water is sucked up through a pipe to the barge, where the liquid and gases are separated. The gas then enters a "scrubber" that separates the methane and carbon dioxide. Ebinger said reducing the overall concentration of gas in the water was a positive move, but warned that more studies were urgently needed to assess the potential environmental impact, especially relating to the unused water and carbon dioxide pumped back into Lake Kivu from the barges.

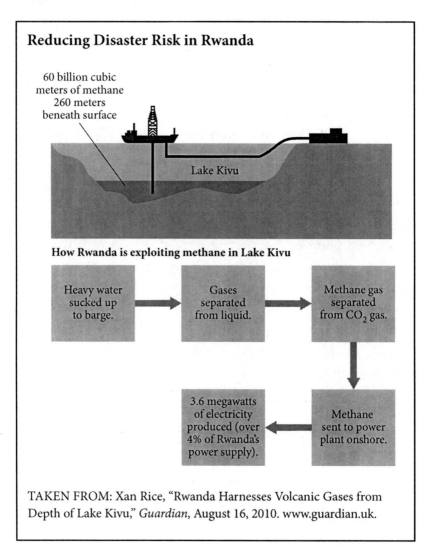

Reducing Disaster Risk in Rwanda

60 billion cubic meters of methane 260 meters beneath surface

Lake Kivu

How Rwanda is exploiting methane in Lake Kivu

Heavy water sucked up to barge. → Gases separated from liquid. → Methane gas separated from CO_2 gas.

↓

3.6 megawatts of electricity produced (over 4% of Rwanda's power supply). ← Methane sent to power plant onshore.

TAKEN FROM: Xan Rice, "Rwanda Harnesses Volcanic Gases from Depth of Lake Kivu," *Guardian*, August 16, 2010. www.guardian.uk.

"With so many projects, if you don't understand everything, you can solve one problem and create three more," she said.

Regardless, Rwanda is proceeding at great speed. Kibuye Power aims to increase its output to 50MW within a few years. A private Rwandan firm is testing the technology on its own barge nearby and has a license to produce a similar amount. And a US company, ContourGlobal, last year [2009] signed a $325m deal with Rwanda to produce 100MW of power from methane.

Talks are also under way with Congo, which has rights to half the natural gas in the lake, about building a joint 200MW plant.

China Effectively Responds to Disasters but Must Improve Risk Reduction

Zhang Qingfeng and Melissa Howell Alipalo

In the following viewpoint, Zhang Qingfeng and Melissa Howell Alipalo report on a study by the Asian Development Bank complimenting China on its "stunningly agile disaster response system" but taking the country to task for not employing more risk-reduction strategies. The writers argue that natural disasters will continue to increase with global warming and that the government must install both monitoring and an early warning system for disasters. Such moves would reduce damage and rebuilding costs. Zhang Qingfeng is the principal water resources specialist at the Asian Development Bank, and Alipalo is a staff consultant to the Asian Development Bank's water and environment operations.

As you read, consider the following questions:

1. What happened at the height of the Yangtze River basin drought?

2. What are the three human and ecological factors named in the viewpoint that will cause disasters to continue to plague China?

Zhang Qingfeng and Melissa Howell Alipalo, "How to Fight Natural Disasters," *China Daily*, June 28, 2011. Reproduced by permission.

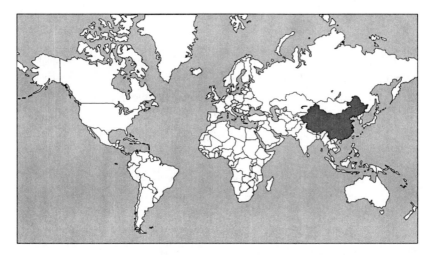

3. What are the six steps of risk management recommended by the writers?

A recent Asian Development Bank (ADB) study on drought management in China says the country has a stunningly agile disaster response system but not a corresponding system of risk reduction and management. In other words, China does not prepare for climate-related disasters; it only reacts to them.

This year [2011], the government has been tackling two prolonged dry spells and the ongoing floods that have caused havoc in central and eastern parts of the country. The second spell of drought in the Yangtze River basin was followed by devastating floods.

At the height of the Yangtze basin drought, 3.5 million people suffered water shortage and cargo shipping was suspended on a 224-kilometer stretch in the middle and lower reaches of the river. The rain that followed came as a relief to people and the parched land in the Yangtze basin, but it also caused deadly landslides in parts of Guizhou and Hunan provinces. Torrential rain and floods have affected 13 provinces, killing almost 100 people and destroying about 27,000 houses.

The economic impact is only beginning to be assessed now that the early rice planting season is likely to be affected. The drought in the northern plains in 2000 was the worst in recent history and cost 47 billion yuan ($7.26 billion) in direct economic loss. The drought in southwest China last year cost 1.4 billion yuan. In June 2010, 27 provinces were hit by floods that caused a direct economic loss of 142.2 billion yuan.

The costs of relief efforts are less well known, but they included hardship allowances, donations by Chinese citizens, and the cost of stabilizing food production and prices.

The Causes of Disasters in China

Such natural disasters will continue to plague the country because of three human and ecological factors. First, the Yangtze River delta region is climate sensitive, for it lies between subtropical and temperate climate zones. From 1951 to 1978, the region was hit by at least one flood or drought or both every two years. Droughts usually occurred in the mountainous areas of the region and floods in the plains.

Greater risk assessment, proper monitoring and an early warning system would greatly reduce the response time and cost—and in turn reduce the damage and rebuilding costs.

Second, according to the national climate change assessment, global warming will increase the frequency of floods and droughts in the region. One of the most striking features of climate change is its impact on the monsoon, which has changed the precipitation pattern. The rainfall pattern in South China has changed, resulting in more floods and making the northern parts more vulnerable to droughts.

Third, ecological degradation has reduced the resilience of ecosystems against the impact of climate change and increased

An Agile Response System and Nonexistent Risk Reduction

While [China] has a finely tuned and sometimes stunningly agile disaster response system, a corresponding system of risk reduction and management does not exist. In effect, the country does not prepare for droughts; it only reacts to them. Infrastructure development may be alleviating some of the symptoms of water shortages, but it is not alleviating the fundamental determinants of shortages or addressing the risks associated with such severe impacts from droughts. The PRC [People's Republic of China] is caught in a reactive mode to droughts and needs to focus policy and resources earlier in the disaster cycle. The country's focus on disaster emergency response should be expanded to *risk* management. Local governments need to understand their "weak spots"—the factors making them particularly vulnerable to droughts—and how to improve their chances by addressing the risk factors.

Qingfeng Zhang, Yoshiaki Kobayashi, Melissa Howell Alipalo,
and Yong Zheng, "Drying Up: What to Do About Droughts in the
People's Republic of China," Asian Development Bank, 2012.

the risk of natural disasters. According to the State Forestry Administration's first large-scale national lake and wetlands survey, more than 1,000 natural lakes and wetlands have disappeared since 1949 and 1.3 million hectares of lake area have been reclaimed for agriculture or urban development.

The growing risk of floods in the central and lower Yangtze River region is partly because floodplains have been usurped for farming, increasing silt deposits in the river.

Natural hazards like droughts and floods cannot be prevented, but we can lessen the damage they cause. Most local governments seem to have missed the opportunity to guard against the impact of natural hazards. The lack of a comprehensive national policy requiring local governments to guard against natural hazards like droughts and floods has aggravated the situation.

China Reacts but Does Not Prepare

Last year, the ADB completed two studies on drought and flood management for China, which said the country's drought management strategy is "stuck" in a reactive mode. China's flood and drought management strategies are similar. They react to emergencies and limit their response until after an emergency has been declared.

If China does not focus its plans to reduce the risks and impact of natural disasters, droughts and floods will continue to cause even greater economic loss.

Greater risk assessment, proper monitoring and an early warning system would greatly reduce the response time and cost—and in turn reduce the damage and rebuilding costs.

China does not have a separate disaster risk management agency. Instead, risk management responsibilities are divided among several agencies, which are brought together through strong central control. The country thus "reacts" to natural hazards instead of focusing its policy and directing its resources to determine disaster cycles.

China's focus on disaster management should be extended to six-step risk management: early warning, monitoring and forecasting; risk assessment; risk mitigation; impact mitigation and emergency responses; recovery, evaluation and contingency planning; and stakeholder participation and public education and awareness.

An integrated approach is critical to creating reserves and enabling ecosystem service to function during droughts and floods and to devise long-term plans. A forthcoming joint publication by ADB, the Ministry of Water Resources and Guiyang city explores a "holistic pathway", using optimal infrastructure, risk management, ecosystem conservation and integrated river basin management.

In China, where climate change is creating unpredictable weather patterns—and thus more droughts and floods—regulating the services provided by ecosystems is important for adapting to climate change and reducing the risks of natural disasters. Examples of such services include climate and water regulation, protection from natural hazards, water and air purification, carbon sequestration, and disease and pest regulation.

If China does not focus its plans to reduce the risks and impact of natural disasters, droughts and floods will continue to cause even greater economic loss.

Periodical and Internet Sources Bibliography

The following articles have been selected to supplement the diverse views presented in this chapter.

AlertNet — "Local Is More Effective, Say Disaster Relief Experts," Thomson Reuters Foundation, October 23, 2009. www.trust.org.

Economist — "Counting the Cost of Calamities: Natural Disasters," January 14, 2012.

Bill Emmott — "The Impact of Disaster," *Newsweek*, March 20, 2011.

Federal Emergency Management Agency (FEMA) — "Crisis Response and Disaster Resilience 2030: Forging Strategic Action in an Age of Uncertainty," January 2012. www.fema.gov.

Katie Hodge — "Africa Aid Delays Are 'Costing Lives,'" *Independent*, January 18, 2012.

Japan Times — "Editorial: Moving Forward with Reconstruction," March 11, 2012.

Libby Powell — "Lost and Found: Families Torn Apart by Conflict Are Being Reunited Through Painstaking Work by the Red Cross," *New Internationalist*, July 2012.

Brian Resnick — "The 2012 Drought's Impact: A Visual Guide," *National Journal*, July 21, 2012.

Manny B. Villar — "Disasters as Challengers, Not Excuses," *Manila Bulletin*, June 12, 2012.

Jason Walsh — "Checklist for Disaster First-Responders: Food, Blankets—and Wi-Fi," *Christian Science Monitor*, August 14, 2012.

For Further Discussion

Chapter 1

1. According to the viewpoints in this chapter, what are some of the major causes of disasters in the world today?

2. What factors change an event from a natural hazard into a disaster, according to the viewpoints in this chapter? In what ways do humans cause events such as an earthquake to become a catastrophe, in the authors' views? Do you agree with these definitions?

Chapter 2

1. According to the viewpoints in this chapter, what roles do social issues such as gender, poverty, political corruption, and violent conflict play in exacerbating human suffering during a disaster? Give specific examples of events that are made significantly worse because of these issues.

2. Why do you think that more women than men die during disasters? Why ought governments attend to gender differences when preparing for and responding to disasters, according to the viewpoints in this chapter?

Chapter 3

1. Why is preparation for disasters so important? What are some of the ideas and models of disaster preparedness offered by the writers in this chapter?

2. Why do governments often fail to adequately prepare for disasters? What are the results of lack of preparation? Use specific examples to illustrate your points. What recent disasters were made worse due to a lack of preparation, according to the writers in this chapter?

Chapter 4

1. According to the viewpoints in this chapter, what is a government's responsibility to its citizens in times of disaster? Likewise, how should the international community respond to a country that has suffered from a serious disaster?

2. In what ways can emergency response from other countries damage the long-term recovery of a country that has suffered a disaster? What seems to be the most helpful and effective way for countries to respond to a disaster in another country? Give examples and note controversies over disaster response.

Organizations to Contact

The editors have compiled the following list of organizations concerned with the issues debated in this book. The descriptions are derived from materials provided by the organizations. All have publications or information available for interested readers. The list was compiled on the date of publication of the present volume; the information provided here may change. Be aware that many organizations take several weeks or longer to respond to inquiries, so allow as much time as possible.

American Red Cross (ARC)

National Headquarters, Washington, DC   20006
(202) 303-4498
e-mail: info@usa.redcross.org
website: www.redcross.org

The American Red Cross (ARC) is part of an international organization that exists to alleviate human suffering in times of emergency. It provides food, shelter, and care to victims of natural and human-made disasters. In addition, it provides education and training in disaster response and preparation. The organization's website includes extensive publications and updates regarding disasters, information about how to prepare for an emergency, and tips for how one can help victims of disasters.

Catholic Relief Services (CRS)

228 W. Lexington Street, Baltimore, MD   21201-3443
(888) 277-7575
website: www.catcholicrelief.org

Catholic Relief Services (CRS) is a Catholic service agency that provides humanitarian assistance throughout the world. In addition, the organization works for emergency preparedness and effective response. The CRS website includes discussions of "complex emergencies," such as intrastate conflicts that result in huge numbers of refugees. In addition, the website provides resources on emergency preparedness, mitigation, and response.

Centre for Research on the Epidemiology of Disasters (CRED)

School of Public Health, Université Catholique de Louvain
Clos Chapelle-aux-Champs, Bte B1.30.15, Brussels   1200
  Belgium
+32 (0)2.764.33.27 • fax: +32 (0)2.764.34.41
website: www.cred.be

Centre for Research on the Epidemiology of Disasters (CRED) is a nonprofit institution in the field of international disaster and conflict health studies. It conducts research and training activities. CRED's website includes descriptions of its projects and many publications including reports such as "Measuring the Human and Economic Impact of Disaster" and articles such as "Civil Nuclear Power at Risk of Tsunamis" and "Famines in Africa: Is Early Warning Early Enough?"

Federal Emergency Management Agency (FEMA)

500 C Street SW, Washington, DC   20472
(202) 646-2500
website: www.fema.gov

The Federal Emergency Management Agency (FEMA) is the US federal agency charged with preparation, response, and mitigation of emergency situations within the United States. FEMA also provides disaster victim assistance. The agency's website includes a blog, videos, photos, news releases, and resources for the study of disasters and advice on keeping safe during emergencies.

Humanitarian Early Warning Service (HEWS)

Inter-Agency Standing Committee
Sub-Working Group on Preparedness
1 United Nations Plaza, New York, NY   10017

(212) 963-5582
website: www.hewsweb.org

Humanitarian Early Warning Service (HEWS) is an inter-agency partnership project that prepares early warnings and forecasts for natural hazards. Early warning information from around the world is collected and analyzed so that HEWS can provide a "one-stop shop for early warning information for all natural hazards." The HEWS website includes special sections on floods, storms, seismic activities, volcanoes, drought, and other natural hazards. In addition, it features a real-time natural hazard map showing risk for natural hazards throughout the world.

Natural Hazards Center
483 UCB, Boulder, Colorado   80309-0483
(303) 492-6818
e-mail: hazctr@colorado.edu
website: www.colorado.edu/hazards/

The Natural Hazards Center at the University of Colorado at Boulder is an academic center dedicated to disseminating knowledge and information concerning disaster preparation, response, and recovery. Its website includes a large database of disaster-related articles, publications, and web resources. It also provides annotated bibliographies of disaster resources and an annotated index by topic, including natural disasters, public health, gender issues, and disaster statistics.

Oxfam America
1100 Fifteenth Street NW, Suite 600, Washington, DC   20005
(800) 776-9326 • fax: (202) 496-1190
website: www.oxfamamerica.org

Oxfam America is an international organization dedicated to the eradication of poverty and injustice. Oxfam also works in emergency situations caused by disasters, such as those caused by the Sahel food crisis in West Africa. Oxfam's website includes descriptions of the organization's projects, a wealth of resource materials, and photographs of places in the world that Oxfam has helped.

Pan American Health Organization (PAHO)
Regional Office, 525 Twenty-Third Street NW
Washington, DC   20037
(202) 974-3000 • fax: (202) 974-3663
website: www.paho.org

The Pan American Health Organization (PAHO) is the regional office of the World Health Organization (WHO). The organization monitors health situations in North and South America and conducts educational and research activities. The group publishes the peer-reviewed journal *Pan American Journal of Public Health*, the report "Health in the Americas," and information notes such as "Food Safety in Natural Disasters."

United Nations Children's Fund (UNICEF)
United States Fund for UNICEF
125 Maiden Lane, 11th Floor, New York, NY   10038
(212) 686-5522
website: www.unicef.org

The United Nations Children's Fund (UNICEF) works to ensure the rights and safety of children around the world. Resources on UNICEF's website include publications such as "UNICEF and Disaster Risk Reduction," "Helping Children Cope with the Stresses of War: A Manual for Parents and Teachers," "The Impact of War on Children," and "Voices of Hope: Adolescents and the Tsunami."

US Agency for International Development (USAID)
Ronald Reagan Building, 1300 Pennsylvania Avenue NW
Washington, DC   20523
(202) 712-4810 • fax: (202) 216-3524
website: www.usaid.gov

The US Agency for International Development (USAID) is the foreign assistance arm of the US government and, as such, is active in responding to disasters and emergencies around the world. USAID's website includes a large number of interesting and helpful articles regarding disasters, such as "Volcanoes Across the Globe," "Before Disaster Strikes," "Anticipating the Worst: Hurricane Preparedness," and "Dual Disasters in Indonesia."

Bibliography of Books

Rick Bissell, ed.   *Preparedness and Response for Cata-strophic Disasters*. Boca Raton, FL: CRC Press, 2013.

David M. Brown   *Gone at 3:17: The Untold Story of the Worst School Disaster in American History*. Dulles, VA: Potomac Books, 2012.

Gregory Button   *Disaster Culture: Knowledge and Un-certainty in the Wake of Human and Environmental Catastrophe*. Walnut Creek, CA: Left Coast Press, 2010.

Marq De Villiers   *The End: Natural Disasters, Manmade Catastrophes, and the Future of Hu-man Survival*. New York: Thomas Dunne Books, 2008.

Florin Diacu   *Megadisasters: The Science of Predict-ing the Next Catastrophe*. Princeton, NJ: Princeton University Press, 2009.

John David Ebert   *The Age of Catastrophe: Disaster and Humanity in Modern Times*. Jeffer-son, NC: McFarland Publishing, 2012.

Brenda Z. Guiberson   *Disasters: Natural and Man-Made Catastrophes Through the Centuries*. New York: Henry Holt and Com-pany, 2010.

| Jed Horne | *Breach of Faith: Hurricane Katrina and the Near Death of a Great American City*. New York: Random House, 2006. |

Edward A. Keller and Duane E. DeVecchio — *Natural Hazards: Earth's Processes as Hazards, Disasters, and Catastrophes*. 3rd ed. New York: Prentice Hall, 2011.

Scott Gabriel Knowles — *The Disaster Experts: Mastering Risk in Modern America*. Philadelphia: University of Pennsylvania Press, 2013.

Eugene Linden — *The Winds of Change: Climate, Weather, and the Destruction of Civilizations*. New York: Simon & Schuster, 2006.

F. Michael Maloof — *A Nation Forsaken: EMP: The Escalating Threat of an American Catastrophe*. Washington, DC: WND Books, 2013.

Bill McGuire — *Global Catastrophes: A Very Short Introduction*. Oxford: Oxford University Press, 2009.

Joel Meyerowitz — *Aftermath*. New York: Phaidon Press, 2006.

Bruce Parker — *The Power of the Sea: Tsunamis, Storm Surges, Rogue Waves, and Our Quest to Predict Disasters*. New York: Palgrave Macmillan, 2010.

Charles Perrow — *The Next Catastrophe: Reducing Our Vulnerabilities to Natural, Industrial, and Terrorist Disasters*. Princeton, NJ: Princeton University Press, 2007.

Amanda Ripley — *The Unthinkable: Who Survives When Disaster Strikes—and Why*. New York: Crown Publishers, 2008.

Carl Safina — *A Sea in Flames: The Deepwater Horizon Oil Blowout*. New York: Crown Publishers, 2011.

Vaclav Smil — *Global Catastrophes and Trends: The Next Fifty Years*. Cambridge, MA: MIT Press, 2008.

Rebecca Solnit — *A Paradise Built in Hell: The Extraordinary Communities That Arise in Disasters*. New York: Viking, 2009.

Matthew Stein — *When Disaster Strikes: A Comprehensive Guide for Emergency Planning and Crisis Survival*. White River Junction, VT: Chelsea Green Publishing, 2011.

Gerald K. Sutton and Joseph A. Cassalli, eds. — *Catastrophe in Japan: The Earthquake and Tsunami of 2011*. Hauppauge, NY: Nova Science Publishers, Inc., 2011.

John Withington — *Disaster!: A History of Earthquakes, Floods, Plagues, and Other Catastrophes*. New York: Skyhorse Publishing, 2010.

Index

Geographic headings and page numbers in **boldface** refer to viewpoints about that country or region.